MY GRANDFATHER,
THORNTON W. BURGESS

MY GRANDFATHER, THORNTON W. BURGESS

An Intimate Portrait

FRANCES B. MEIGS

Commonwealth Editions
Beverly, Massachusetts

To my children and grandchildren, with love

Library of Congress Cataloging-in-Publication Data
Meigs, Frances B., 1922–
    My grandfather, Thornton W. Burgess : an intimate portrait / Frances B. Meigs
       p. com.
    ISBN 1-889833-05-3 (alk. paper)
    1. Burgess, Thornton W. (Thornton Waldo), 1874–1965 -- Family. 2. Authors, American -- Family relationships. 3. Grandfathers -- United States -- Biography. 4. Meigs, Frances B., 1922– -- Family. 5. Children's stories -- Authorship. 6. Nature stories -- Authorship. I. Title.
    PS3503.U6075Z76 1998
    813'.52--dc21
    [B]   98-00000
                                             CIP

Designed by Joyce C. Weston.

Commonwealth Editions is an imprint of
Memoirs Unlimited, 21 Lothrop Street, Beverly, Mass. 01915.

Printed in the United States of America.

Contents

Grateful acknowledgment is made to the following for their permission to use photographs:

The Boston Globe (staff photo): page 136 (top)

Nancy Burgess Hughes, pages 41 and 132.

Life magazine (Eric Schall photos): frontispiece and pages 46 (top) and 134.

Thornton W. Burgess Society, East Sandwich, Massachusetts: pages 42 (bottom), 43, 44, 45, 48, 135 (top and bottom), and 136 (bottom).

All other photographs are from the author's collection.

Acknowledgments

I am grateful to the many friends and family who encouraged me during the long process of writing this book and most especially for the loving support of my husband, Charles; my children, Carolyn and Kathryn; and those who constantly jogged my memory, my brother Robert and sister Rosemary.

I am particularly grateful to my dear friend Edward Myers, who read and critiqued the awkward beginnings of my first draft and gave me the confidence to continue, and to Charlotte Winslow for her advice. Appreciation also goes to Gwen Brown, the former curator of the Thornton W. Burgess Society, for the many hours we spent together poring over the letters, diaries, and articles written by and about Thornton Burgess; to Jeanne Johnson, director of the Society, whose office we shared; and to Kristine Hastreiter, the present curator, for her invaluable help in gathering photographs and other important material. Doug Kimball, director of the Massachusetts Audubon Sanctuary at Laughing Brook in Hampden, has been a constant friend and aid in securing information, photographs, and access to the Burgess files there. To Nancy Burgess Hughes, I give thanks for her friendship and the generosity with which she shared her memories.

I wish to express my deep appreciation and gratitude to the people who so kindly read my manuscript and gave so generously of their comments: Bradford Washburn of the Boston Museum of Science; Paul Brooks, author; Cleveland Amory, author; John Mitchell, author and editor of the journal of the Massachusetts Audubon Society; and Nancy Titcomb of the Burgess Society in Sandwich.

I also wish to thank my friend and publisher Webster Bull and Susanna Brougham, who edited this book, for their intuitive and discriminating confidence in my intent.

—Bedford, Massachusetts, spring 1998

MY GRANDFATHER,
THORNTON W. BURGESS

Around the Toll Road a way, and into a town, and up a great hill, and around a long curve, a noisy little brook tumbles out of the hills and chuckles past a little gray house. I call it "Laughing Brook." It empties into the Scantic River and I guess it has a real name, but I've forgotten it.

—*Thornton W. Burgess*

Prologue

*H*E WAS AN OLD MAN. Wrapped in a blanket, he sat in a wheelchair beside the brook that flowed past the gray shingled eighteenth-century home on his farm in Hampden, just east of Springfield, Massachusetts. The house was empty, for those who had lived there had gone before him. It was 1965.

He could no longer hear Laughing Brook, the songs of the birds he knew so well, the peepers that heralded the spring. But in the silence of his thoughts, he no doubt recalled these sounds and felt the abiding presence of the ones he had loved long ago. He could hear singing and the laughter of children. He could smell new-mown grass, the sweet fragrance of flowers, wood burning in the fireplaces, and the tantalizing aroma of cooking in the kitchen.

As he watched the brook cascading over the rocks, tumbling down from the purple hills on its journey toward the sea, and saw the leaves of the great elms rustling in the soft breeze, did he wonder what would become of this beautiful place, so small yet so priceless a part of the vast universe, after he was gone? Perhaps the words of a favorite psalm gave him reassurance: "I will lift up mine eyes unto the hills, from whence cometh my help." He understood his connectedness to all things passing and to come, as expressed so beautifully by Rachel Carson in describing the loveliest voice in the forest—that of the hermit thrush: "Its phrases were filled with a beauty and a meaning that was not wholly of the present, as though the thrush were singing of other sunsets, extending far beyond his personal memory through eons of time when his forbears had known this place."

Joyous all the winds that blow To the heart with love aglow.

A quizzical smile, revealing his undaunted optimism, spread across this man's face, sparking a twinkle in his eyes. He turned slowly and beckoned to his nurse that it was time for him to leave his beloved home for the last time and return to the nursing home a mile downstream, where he could watch this same brook meandering by his window.

This man was Thornton Waldo Burgess, the most widely read author of children's nature stories in the United States from 1910 to 1950 and my grandfather. After he died on June 5, 1965, at the age of ninety-one, and after my own children had grown, married, and had children of their own,

I began to read again his autobiography, *Now I Remember.* These recollections, his diaries and letters, and my own memories have helped me recall and reconstruct much of his life.

Grandpa, as I affectionately called him, was loved and admired by the millions of people whom he reached through his books, his daily column in the *New York Herald Tribune* and many other newspapers across the country, and his pioneering contributions to conservation and environmentalism. Predominantly through his children's books—simple, whimsical narratives and moral lessons taught by the likes of Reddy Fox, Jimmy Skunk, Peter Rabbit, Johnny Chuck, and Sammy Jay—he instilled in readers his sense of the awe and wonder of creation and the ineffable mystery of the creator. But rather than romanticize or idealize nature, he bestowed on both children and adults his detailed knowledge of the natural world gained from close study and research. An early environmentalist, he raised the consciousness of millions, a legacy that is still alive today.

Although he appeared happiest when solitary, Grandpa showed genuine interest and care for other people, particularly for those close to him. He had a friendly attitude and an optimistic view of life. My brother and sisters and I were raised to a great extent by our grandparents. We lived with them much of the time and eagerly awaited our return whenever we were separated. As a child, I did not always understand Grandpa, but I loved him very much and depended upon him for strength and support. As I grew older, I marveled at his resilience and goodness.

So much has been written and told about him that I am often asked, "What was he really like?"

I reply: "He was all the extraordinary things you have imagined him to be. He led an exceptionally full and productive life, surrounded by family and friends. He cared deeply for others and had an intuitive gift for endearing himself to children through his humor and wisdom. But he was often bewildered by the ironies of his life, especially his relationship with his only natural child, Thornton W. Burgess III."

Previously, I had thought that to mention anything imperfect or painful about my grandfather's life might somehow mar the image cherished by his public audience and might invade the privacy and breach the loyalties that we as a family hold close. But I think differently now, and I wish to tell the story of Thornton Burgess as I knew him.

Chapter One

*T*HORNTON WALDO BURGESS was born in a large white clapboard house, with a wide porch spanning the front, at 6 School Street in Sandwich, Massachusetts, the oldest town on Cape Cod. He was born on January 14, 1874, nine years after the end of the Civil War. His American ancestry can be traced to 1637 and Thomas Burgess, one of the original settlers in Sandwich. Grandpa was of the ninth generation.

His father, Thornton W. Burgess, Sr., died when he was only nine months old, leaving his mother, Caroline Frances Haywood Burgess, a widow. Caroline had been left an orphan with her younger sister, Lucy, at the age of four and had grown up in the home of her uncle Charles C. P. Waterman, who was her mother's brother. Lucy had gone to live with other relatives in another part of the state. After Thornton Burgess, Sr., died, Caroline's uncle Charles, who was very fond of her, asked her to live with him again where she had grown up, at 170 Main Street in Sandwich.

The young Thornton W. Burgess became very fond of his "grandfather," as he called his great-uncle Charles, and told of their adventures together. The most familiar was the tale of the great striped whale. For the people of Sandwich and a small boy of five years old, the arrival of this whale was an exciting event. It left a vivid and enduring image in Grandpa's mind.

Two whales had been harpooned off Provincetown, which lies about twenty-five miles from Sandwich directly across Cape Cod Bay. Both whales were believed to be fatally wounded, but one, the great blue whale, had made its way to Sandwich, where it had grounded in shallow tidal waters off the beach. When

No home is ever mean or poor
Where love awaits you at the door.

Grandpa arrived with his cousin—each boy holding tightly to one of Great-uncle Charles's hands, the March wind blowing hard, the gulls screaming overhead, and the flying sand sting-ing their faces—they saw a huge whale lying there. Harpoons had pierced its lungs, and it had drowned. Whalemen sur-rounded it, using their flensing knives to cut long strips of the whale's blubber down to the red flesh beneath.

The whale was no longer a beautiful shiny gray, blue, or black; it was, in my grandfather's words, "red and white striped." Loading their boats with the blubber, which, when melted down, would become valuable lamp oil, the whalemen rowed it out to the ship through the rough white-capped waves and continued to row back and forth to get more. This great blue leviathan of the deep, the largest known of all the whales, was said to have measured seventy-four feet in length.

To Grandpa as a small boy, this mutilated gentle giant looked like a huge red-and-white-striped barber's pole. For the rest of his life, any mention of the great whales would conjure up the mixed emotions of this memory: great sorrow for the death of the whale and admiration for the strength and endurance shown by the whalemen as they worked on that stormy March morning.

One summer morning when my grandfather was nearly six, his great-uncle Charles had a surprise for him. He led him to the back of the house to see the new swing he had hung from a horizontal branch of the old apple tree. It was a wonderful surprise, as Grandpa was not used to receiving presents or gifts of unnecessary value which did not bring grist to the mill, so to speak. His mother was always struggling to make ends meet.

A home is always what you make it; With love there you will ne'er forsake it.

In 1880, before Grandpa reached his seventh birthday, he and his mother moved to his paternal grandparents' house at 5 Jarves Street in Sandwich. They had to move because the health of Great-uncle Charles had started to fail. In 1882 the Jarves Street house was sold as Grandpa's grandparents, Charles Henry and Ann Swift Nye Burgess, moved to Colorado Springs, and Grandpa and his mother moved again. Altogether they were obliged to seek new lodgings about ten times while in Sandwich.

Things were especially difficult because Grandpa's mother, Caroline, was a semi-invalid with a weak heart. But with the help of his grandparents, mother and son managed to support themselves. Caroline made candy, which Grandpa peddled from house to house and sold to the laborers in the Sandwich glassworks. In the winter he shoveled snow for pay, and in the springtime he picked and sold dandelion greens and bunches of the wild pink trailing arbutus, his favorite flower and now an endangered species.

He picked the first blueberries of summer in July, and in the fall he picked cranberries, a crop so important to the Cape Cod economy that school did not start until October. Later he described what cranberry-picking was like in his early years:

> In those days, the scoop and rake were outlawed. Picking was a job for nimble fingers. The bogs were lined off in rows by means of white cord. They were full of kneeling figures, the girls and women sunbonneted, and the men and boys for the most part in old trousers and flannel shirts. Whole families went cranberrying. Some bogs were not far back of the beach sand dunes; some were in deep woods near the shores of ponds. There was time for

picnic lunches and the spice of good stories and old famil-
iar songs.

Cranberry picking was hard on the hands. We boys
used shoemaker's wax to protect the quick or base of each
fingernail. Girls often wore gloves. But even though they
beat us picking, we boys scorned gloves. Cranberries on
the cape are a bigger and more important crop than ever,
but no longer are they "picked," while the communal and
social life of long-ago days have been "scooped" away.

At the end of the day there was always the long walk
or ride home, sometimes a matter of several miles, a jar-
ring ride on boards put across the sides of a blue truck
wagon drawn by a plodding horse or a span (a two-horse
team) which plodded and sometimes hurried with a jolt-
ing trot.

By the time he was twelve years old, Grandpa was able to
buy all his own clothes. To supplement his berry- and flower-
picking business, he delivered eggs and milk in the neighborhood, pulling the goods along in his small wood-slatted wagon.
He also walked for miles delivering mail and telegrams to the
outskirts of town, for there were no telephones in those days.

Grandpa drove other people's cows daily to and from pasture. From colonial times until recent years, Sandwich had a
public pasture called Town Neck, bordering the sea near the
present entrance to the Cape Cod Canal. From spring until
fall, village folk with one or two cows, and others on the edge

of the village with small herds but with no available pasture-land would drive their cows there. Grandpa drove two small herds comprising eight to twelve cows to the neck from these adjoining farms, a distance of over a mile. He drove them to pasture shortly after six o'clock in the morning, and at four o'clock in the afternoon—when the cows gathered to be let out and the gate was opened—he cut his cows from the herd and drove them home.

On the way home one day, he realized that one of his cows was missing. There was nothing to do but drive the others home and then trudge back to look for the missing one. A thunderstorm was brewing, and he didn't like thunderstorms. He was frightened but knew he had to find the missing cow. Rain began to fall, accompanied by loud claps of thunder and electric sizzles of lightning. He could hear the dull booming of the surf beyond the dunes and the wild screaming of the gulls.

Wet to the skin, the ten-year-old searched as best he could for his lost cow. Town Neck was a vast lonely area with patches of brush, swampy places, and two or three small freshwater ponds. Finally, to his relief he found his missing cow lying behind some brush. Beside her was a newborn calf. Excited and relieved, he ran back to get the farmer's wagon to carry the calf and lead its mother home. He said his own mother was happy to see him that night and to hear of his adventure. She didn't mind a bit that he was late for supper.

One year when Grandpa was a boy, he received a bow gun for Christmas. The propelling force of the gun was provided by stout rubber bands, similar to those of a slingshot. This pleased him very much, as all his chums had bow guns. "Proudly," as he later described it, "I sallied forth that winter to hunt. I shot a chickadee. Poor little Tommy Tit! [as he referred to him in his stories] I still see him held out in a grimy hand for my mother to look at, the mighty hunter flushed with pride at this proof of his marksmanship."

Who has attentive ear or eye Will learn a lot if he will try.

As he grew older he devoured stories of hunting and fishing. He went afield in woods or on the marshes at every opportunity, studying the wild things and their ways so that he might better outwit and kill them. He was unaware that he was laying the foundation for his life's work, which began when he put away the gun for camera and typewriter. "Through the years," he wrote in his autobiography, "I have sought to expiate that tragic shot of long ago by striving to teach children to love and protect our birds and animals."

While a high school student, Grandpa raised a red-tailed hawk, one of the largest of the so-called hen hawks. Years later he told us that he had originally written this story for *Good Housekeeping* under the name of W. B. Thornton.

I got him from a nest when he was abandoned and only partly feathered out. I brought him up on a diet of frogs, raw meat, fish, and my neighbor's chickens. He grew into a handsome, great bird. I kept him in a shed nights, taking him out each morning to a post in the yard to which he was tied by a stout string fastened to a leather thong about one leg. I used to transfer him from shed to post by means of a short stick on which he would perch while I carried him out. Occasionally he would choose my wrist instead of the stick, and then there was nothing for it but to walk very straight and hold the arm very steady, for his huge talons were capable of tearing my wrist to shreds, and if my arm was a bit unsteady, for he was a heavy fellow, he had an uncomfortable way of tightening his grip to retain his balance.

A neighbor's hen yard was a source of perpetual interest. Several times before he was old enough for extended flight, he broke his tether and dined at my neighbor's expense. Later, as he attained maturity, he would sit for hours gazing off into space until I was moved to pity his captive wild heart. But he was witless, and though he obtained his liberty he knew not what to do with it.

Coming home one noon I found a broken cord and no hawk. Presently I discovered him silhouetted against the sky over the ridge pole of a distant barn. He saw me and recognized me before I reached the barn, and cursed me vigorously in the shrill screaming vernacular of the hawk tribe. As I worked my way up the roof he did a side step along the ridge pole, the small feathers on the top of his head raised in an angry pompadour, screaming fiercely meantime. As I approached he struck viciously with his huge talons, his curved beak, and strong wings, but made no attempt to fly away. So I gathered him up, slid down the roof, and carried him home.

Once again I found him gone. This time he had chosen a high tower, climbing which was out of the question. Searching the neighborhood I got a bit of raw meat, and then sought a field near the tower. No sooner did I hold up the meat than his keen eye saw it, and he launched himself from the tower like a feathered thunderbolt. Quite needless to say I was content to drop the meat on the ground. A second later he pounced upon it. Then, as before, he fought vigorously against being retaken, but made no effort to fly away.

Other feathered friends I have had: pigeons so timid when I got them that they would taste no food while anyone was near, but later would sit on my hand and take corn from between my lips; wild sea birds brought to me wounded to be nursed; shy little ones who came to love the hand which fed them.

Although it was tragic that Grandpa hadn't known his father, I think he believed that he'd had a wonderful childhood. It never occurred to him that he lacked for anything. He had his mother and grandparents, his aunts, uncles, cousins, and friends—and the whole world of nature to explore.

His autobiography contains happy memories of growing up in Sandwich, "where I had first felt the wind-whipped sand of the shore bite and sting, the beach grass cut, and where I had learned that life was hard: but where the sky was blue and the air was soft. It was where the real and the unreal met, and the impossible became probable. I could feel the excitement and thrill of my first field observation. It was where the pattern of my life was set."

When Grandpa graduated from Sandwich High School in 1891, he took a job in a local grocery store while his mother continued with her candy business. Grandpa's paternal grandfather, Charles Burgess, a retired merchant who had been helping to support him and his mother, could see little practical value in higher education. But he still offered to finance Grandpa for one term at a commercial school in Boston.

*When things go bad
and life is rough,
Advantage lies in being
tough.*

Grandpa and his mother then moved together to an apartment in Somerville from which he commuted to Boston by horsecar, since the electric trolley did not extend as far as Somerville. He enrolled in the commercial school and spent the winter trying to master bookkeeping. At the end of his term he got a job as cashier and assistant book-keeper at Jameson and Knowles Company, Importers and Retailers of Fine Shoes, at 15 Winter Street in Boston. Occasionally, when there was a shortage of salesmen, he helped out on the floor. He was extremely unhappy with this job and felt miserably out of place. He had not yet figured out what he wanted to do with his life. Like a tree transplanted to an inhospitable environment, he longed for the peace and quiet of the country. As a result, he always had understanding and sympathy for anyone "who has not yet found himself when he starts out in the world." He remembered his own "period of the yet undiscovered self" as a time of loneliness and darkness.

Soon Grandpa's mother was no longer well enough to continue housekeeping, so she moved to Springfield, Massachusetts, to live with her sister, Lucy, and thus they were reunited after a long separation. (Lucy had married and had a child named Willie.) Grandpa secured a small bedroom in a private home in Somerville. He and his boyhood friend Ernest, then attending MIT, and other old friends attending Harvard began to spend time together. Grandpa had always dreamed of going to college and at the time felt that he was missing out on a great deal because he didn't have the money to attend. Years later he would think better of having missed the opportunity: "It was for the best. I can see how I might easily have fallen under the influence of teachers who might have changed my whole outlook and style. This way I had to work out my own salvation."

When the Jameson and Knowles shoe store cut back on its help, Grandpa was out of a job. He began scanning the want ads and making rounds at employment agencies. One day on impulse, he bought a few lines of space in a small newspaper devoted to advertising, called *Brains*. Grandpa often wrote poems and rhymes for his own amusement, but now he hung out his shingle:

SAVE TIME LABOR AND TROUBLE
Get a good man
That can wield a good pen;
Let him advertise for you
Tho' it cost you a ten!
And in that way
you will save all three.
Try my work,
and if not satisfactory,
just return it.
Ads in rhyme a specialty.

Of this small beginning he said, "It was preposterous. It was absurd. Of course it was, and still is, inconceivable that that little investment drawn from my meager capital should pay off in hard cash, but it did. Moreover, it paid a tremendous extra dividend in that it definitely settled for all time the question of what I wanted to do. I wanted to write. From that time on I knew that I must somehow make my living with my pen. There was not even a shadow of doubt."

As soon as that issue of *Brains* was off the press, Grandpa received a request to call at an advertising agency in Boston. The agency was doing some advertising for the Miles Standish Spring Water Company. They wanted him to paraphrase Longfellow's epic of Miles Standish, reduce it to twenty short verses, and insert the discovery of a spring into the poem.

His friend Ernest came to his room that evening and listened critically while Grandpa read his efforts aloud. He nodded approval and asked, "How much are you going to ask for it?"

"I think I ought to get five dollars for it," Grandpa responded.

"You're crazy," Ernest said. "Don't ask a cent less than fifteen."

Grandpa got his fifteen dollars, much to his surprise, after mumbling his request to the president of the company. He never did acquire a liking for the business part of his work; neither was he ever very good at it. He was grateful for Ernest's advice, but the two of them always wondered what the agency had expected to pay for the verses.

Grandpa continued to write verse and now and then a bit of prose in an effort to satisfy his growing desire for a job where he might at least "smell the printer's ink." Yet the only jobs he was able to get required the hated bookkeeping, which he performed reluctantly while dreaming of working for a publishing house. Then, just before Thanksgiving in 1895, a special-delivery letter came from his mother in Springfield. She had just learned from her neighbor that the office boy in the editorial rooms of the Phelps Publishing Company had recently been discharged.

On his mother's advice, at age twenty-one Grandpa went to Springfield where he was introduced to the editor in chief of Phelps, who told him to arrive at the publishing company at seven-thirty the following morning. Grandpa was elated, even though he was to sweep the editorial rooms, dust the desks and chairs, sharpen the pencils of all the editors, empty the wastebaskets, and collect the mail and distribute it. By the time these things were done, someone would instruct him in additional duties. For the remainder of the day he would be at the beck and call of the editors. When he saw his mother after his interview, he proudly told her, "I am now on the lowest rung of the ladder, but I am on the ladder."

Soon he began to offer items of news he had picked up, and as time went on he contributed more and more, until he was not only editorial office boy and janitor, but also a cub reporter. When the Phelps company took over *Good Housekeeping* magazine, he became a sort of editorial utility man. He said, "I remember one issue had stories by me under four different names!" A series of his monthly feature articles were put together in book form and called *The Bride's Primer* over his by-line. It was written with humor and a bit tongue-in-cheek, since he was unmarried, male, and knew little of the subject at hand. All the same, it was a milestone for him. "Now," he said, "I am at least a recognized author." In 1902 he wrote a four-page outdoor calendar for *Good Housekeeping,* with little essays about the outdoors, the weather, and so on.

In 1905 Grandpa purchased a house at 61 Washington Road in Springfield where he and his mother could at last have a permanent home. It was a large, three-story frame house in the quiet outskirts of town, set back about a hundred feet from a wide, tree-lined street. The house was situated near enough to New York and Boston, "not too near either," he said, "but near one of the most beautiful city parks in all America—Forest Park." The park was only three minutes' walk from his doorstep, a place where he liked to wander, often taking his fishing pole. He watched the countless birds that stopped there to break the long semi-annual migrations between summer nesting places and winter retreats in the sunny South.

True independence he has known Whose home has been his very own.

That summer Grandpa married Nina E. Osborne of West Springfield. Less than a year later, while giving birth to their son, Thornton W. Burgess III, Nina died. Grief-stricken, Grandpa sought refuge in his work, and with the help of his mother and her sister Lucy, he found care for his son sometimes with some of Lucy's family in Illinois.

While young Thornton, not yet three years old, was away in Illinois, Grandpa thought of him constantly. He began writing him stories each night and sending them in the mail. These stories told of what he had seen and heard out in the meadows and fields, on the hills, and along the streams. Some, he explained, were stories about Old Mother West Wind "who came down from the Purple Hills in the golden light of the early morning. Over her shoulders was slung a bag—a great big bag—and in the bag were all of Old Mother West Wind's children, the Merry Little Breezes." Old Mother West Wind and her offspring had told him about Reddy Fox, Peter Rabbit, Jerry Muskrat, Hooty the Owl, and all the other little furred and feathered folk. She told him that they had exciting adventures and made mistakes just like any little boy. Grandpa published some of these same stories in *Good Housekeeping* magazine.

Soon a representative from Little, Brown and Company of Boston asked that Grandpa send as many of these stories as he could for consideration as a possible book. Much to Grandpa's delight, *Old Mother West Wind* was published in the fall of 1910. The publishers asked for another book the following year, and *Mother West Wind's Children* rolled off the press. Although these books launched Grandpa on his career of writing children's books, the royalties did not amount to very much, so he was glad to have a steady income from *Good*

Housekeeping. He still could not imagine that his life's work would be writing children's stories.

Grandpa's good friend the well-known entomologist Willis Grant Johnson had become chief editor of the Orange Judd Company, associated with Phelps Publishing, both leaders in agricultural publications. Among their periodicals were *Farm and Home, American Agriculturist, Orange Judd Farmer,* and *New England Homestead.* The company also published an illustrated weekly newspaper called the *Springfield Homestead.* This publication was devoted to social news and activities, with articles of special interest to Springfield and its vicinity. Grandpa became the *Homestead's* photographer and soon wrote stories to go with the photographs. He eventually became a part-time reporter, contributing verse and short articles to the household departments of the Orange Judd Company's various farm papers. Now and then he was allowed the occasional column of his own.

Then Willis Johnson died suddenly from spinal meningitis, leaving his wife, Fannie, with two children: Chester, age fourteen, and Helen (my mother), age nine. In 1911, after a two-year courtship, Grandpa married my grandmother in Ithaca, New York. Thus he became my stepgrandfather, but in reality the only grandfather I ever knew. My grandmother Fannie, whom we called Nanna, was a beauty. Strong of mind and body, she had a small girlish figure, delicate features, and a sweet, radiant smile. She had soft, long brown hair, which she piled up loosely around her head, keeping it in place with combs and hairpins. Her surprising sense of humor caught one off guard with its quickness. She was full of fun, warm, and loving. She and Grandpa shared many interests. For example, they enjoyed fishing and camping together, particularly in New Brunswick, where they were often joined by many friends. Looking at pictures of them in those days, I can't help but admire the happiness in their faces and the evident complementarity of their spirits—right down to the way they dressed. If one was wearing a four-in-hand tie or bow tie, so was the other. Grandpa's nickname for her was "Lady."

After the marriage, Nanna and her two children moved to Washington Road to live with Grandpa, his mother Caroline, and young Thornton, who had come home to Springfield. Disharmony reigned as the two women tried to run the house and raise the children together. Grandpa kept his office on the third floor, where he worked long hours when not away from home and kept himself clear of domestic affairs below. He knew something of the discord, but with his usual good-natured optimism, he felt it would be resolved in time.

To compound these domestic problems, *Good Housekeeping* was sold to a New York publisher a few months after Grandpa and Nanna's marriage, and after fifteen years with the magazine he was given two weeks' notice. The period that followed was difficult for the entire family: one week there might be twenty-five dollars from the sale of a story, the next week nothing. To make ends meet, Grandpa found temporary employment with the advertising department of the J. H.

McFarland Company in Harrisburg, Pennsylvania. He spent the summer of 1911 in Harrisburg away from his family, writing catalogue, magazine, and mail-order copy.

In late fall of that year he received a letter asking that he submit educational children's stories to a new syndicate, the Associated Newspapers, which included the *Chicago Daily News*, the *Kansas City Star*, the *Philadelphia Bulletin*, the *New York Globe*, and the *Boston Globe*. Grandpa signed a contract to write six stories a week for six months, at thirty-five dollars a week. At the end of six months, if the stories were successful, the contract would be renewed at fifty dollars per week. However, for financial security, he kept his advertising job with J. H. McFarland Company, which sent him to Florida for one month in the spring of 1912 to make photographs and secure material for catalogues and booklets.

Much to Grandpa's sorrow, in 1912 his mother died. Her struggle to supply both economic and emotional support during his early years left an indelible impression on him. "Whatever of success I may have attained," Grandpa would say, "I owe in large measure to my mother—her careful training, her courage, her understanding of my love of nature, her loving sympathy with my boyish pursuits, her ambition for my future life, her faith."

His mother's death left Grandpa alone with Nanna and the three children, now age nineteen, fourteen, and six. Young Thornton had become angry and rebellious in response to the insecurity, losses, and upheavals he had already suffered in his young life, and Nanna became frustrated by his behavior. Tragically, the little boy came to resent her. No matter how she tried to please or comfort him, or how much she scolded or punished him, nothing seemed to make a difference, and Grandpa was too busy to be of much assistance.

One winter day young Thornton made Nanna so upset that she shut him out of the house. His tantrum attracted the attention of a neighbor, who called the police and reported what seemed to be cruel punishment on Nanna's part. The matter was immediately turned over to the Society for the Prevention of Cruelty to Children, and, much to the family's horror, news of the incident was published in the Springfield newspapers.

For Nanna and Grandpa the pain and embarrassment were overwhelming. Filled with feelings of guilt and sorrow, Grandpa blamed himself and his long absences from home for Thornton's problems. It was agreed shortly thereafter that the boy should again go to live with relatives, at least for a while. Grandpa still needed to gain financial security, and his work continued to take him away from home for lengthy periods. But he prayed hard that when he became an established author with a good steady income, things would be different; he would have more time to spend with his family, and his little son could come back to live with them.

With a neophyte's elation and his own lack of business sense, Grandpa had signed his contract with Associated

Newspapers without seeking legal advice. He believed the syndicate was buying only first serial rights, with all other rights retained by him. However, in the written contract, the word *first* had been omitted, a subtlety Grandpa didn't notice. Therefore when Grandpa's first syndicated story with Associated appeared in February 1912, he had a rude surprise. Representatives of the syndicate claimed they had bought all serial rights and could reprint and sell Grandpa's stories as often as they desired, without offering any remuneration to him.

That same year, a publisher approached Grandpa and asked that he write a book for the Boy Scouts. (Baron Baden-Powell, founder of the Boy Scouts, had published the first Boy Scout manual in 1908.) *The Boy Scouts of Woodcraft Camp* by Thornton W. Burgess became an immediate success. Three more Boy Scout books followed, and by 1913 he was devoting all his time to writing the daily stories and his books, including another volume in the Old Mother West Wind series. His workload was increased by invitations to lecture, sometimes addressing two or three thousand children in a single audience. At long last, Grandpa gave up the advertising field.

Now feeling financially secure for perhaps the first time in his life, Grandpa brought young Thornton home to live with the family and attend school in Springfield. Grandpa could at last spend more time at home with his family and write in his own office on the third floor. Yet as much as Grandpa loved him, coming home was no panacea for the problems of his son. Young Thornton continued to be unhappy and rebellious.

Grandpa grew to love his stepdaughter Helen as though she were his own daughter. She was gentle and loving, with a beautiful smile that she gave away freely. She adored her stepfather—Dad, as she called him—and liked to help her mother, Fannie, cook his favorite meals. When she was young, she played with the many beautiful china dolls she had collected over the years, and she talked to Grandpa about them as though they were real. Helen gave them charming names such as Isadora, Cinderella, Penelope, and Rosalinda, and Grandpa entered into the make-believe dialogue that actually addressed real-life joys and sorrows, attributing them to the dolls. Through the magic of their imaginations, they watched Peter Rabbit go "lipperty, lipperty, lip" down the crooked little path. Helen was always happy with her Dad, and as she grew older they shared an abiding, caring affection that lasted all their lives. He always spoke of her as "my very dear daughter."

Sticks will break and sticks will bend, And all things bad will have an end.

In 1916 some of Grandpa's friends and editors suggested that he write a bird book for children. The project would involve a great deal of research to select the birds most likely to be seen by the greatest number of children across the United States, and then to portray these birds accurately in appearance and habits. The book was to be both a storybook and an authoritative handbook. Louis Agassiz Fuertes, the great artist and naturalist, was commissioned to illustrate the volume. After graduating from Garland Finishing School in Boston, my mother, Helen, helped Grandpa as his secretary while he wrote *The Burgess Bird Book for Children*.

Published by Little, Brown and Company in 1919, *The Burgess Bird Book for Children* was at once a best-seller. Wrote William Hornaday, director of the New York Zoological Society, "It rings true and is by far the best bird book for children that we have ever seen. In fact it is the very book that anxious mothers, children, and booksellers have all been waiting for, for twenty years." *The Bird Book* was followed later by *The Animal Book, The Flower Book,* and *The Seashore Book,* which also presented natural history in an accurate and entertaining form.

During this same period, Grandpa was introduced to Harrison Cady, an illustrator commissioned to illustrate some of Grandpa's stories for the *People's Home Journal*. Grandpa was completely captivated by Cady's style and humor, and a collaboration began that would evolve into a close friendship lasting nearly half a century. Cady produced about fifteen thousand drawings for Grandpa's stories in the daily press alone, and thousands more for his many books. In later years, Grandpa would say that a great portion of his own popularity was due to the distinction of Harrison Cady's illustrations.

The childhood, background, and early career struggles of both Grandpa and his illustrator-friend have many parallels. Early in youth, each became attuned to nature—the author in Sandwich, where he reveled in the beauty of sand dunes and sea, salt marshes, and cranberry bogs, and the illustrator in his birthplace of Gardner, Massachusetts, where he explored the meadows, the woods, and an old mill pond with its dragonflies, grandfather frogs, and lily pads. Three years younger than Grandpa, Cady would recall his father taking him for walks in the woods surrounding their home, lifting a rock, and saying, "This is somebody's home." In his mind's eye the boy Cady saw little Johnny Beetle, complete with shiny waistcoat and top hat.

The family of each man doubted that either would make much of a livelihood. Time, though, vindicated their independent choice of careers. And like the successful little woodchuck in Grandpa's favorite story about Johnny Chuck's search for "The Best Thing in the World," Grandpa and Cady eventually found the same prize, love.

Cady started his own quest as a young newspaper illustrator, with walking stick, black slouch hat, and a press badge worn proudly. Working for the *New York Herald* and later the *Brooklyn Eagle,* he covered courtroom trials, parties, horse shows, yacht races—all sorts of things that would be covered by a press photographer today. "It was a wonderful experience for a country boy," he would say. "It didn't pay too much at first, and for a while I supported my mother and myself on ten dollars a week. But we loved New York, and my mother felt that it was like living in the Arabian Nights with everything free."

John Ames Mitchell, editor of the old *Life* magazine, was attracted to Cady's artistic talents and whimsical humor and hired him as staff artist, a position he held for twenty-three years, drawing everything from bugs and animals to highlights of World War I and powerful visual commentaries on social problems. (The old *Life*, a weekly, was the American counterpart of *Punch*, the British humor magazine.) Mitchell himself was a fine artist and writer as well as a superb editor; he knew politics, art, and literature and attracted some of the best names in the country to his staff. Once a week the artists and writers would meet with him, after which they would retire to the King's Tap House where they would "dine in state." This combination of good food, good wines, and good conversation led to the formation of the famous Dutch Treat Club. The names of the original members, who numbered fewer than twenty, read like a library list. They included Irvin Cobb, Frank Mellon, G. K. Chesterton, Joseph Conrad, Arthur Conan Doyle, H. G. Wells, and Dana Gibson. Cady also enjoyed the company of Mark Twain, Theodore Roosevelt, Frances Hodgson Burnett, and other literary lights.

A New York critic, reviewing Cady's one-man show at the

Salmagundi Club, wrote: "Primarily a draftsman, Cady uses his brush like a pen. So these pictures can be read like a storybook. And, as his colors are fresh, it is very agreeable reading." Reminded that he liked to put dogs and boys in his paintings, Cady chuckled, "Well, I guess that's right. You see, that Gardner boyhood put a pattern on my life. Like Peter Pan, I never grew up."

Cady was blessed with an extraordinary personality. Many remember his famous yarns, told so convincingly that an unwary listener was easily tricked into believing that he had been runner-up in the world's whittling sweepstakes or that he owned bustles worn by Queen Victoria, Jenny Lind, and Mrs. Tom Thumb. Most notable of all ladies in his life was his beloved wife, Melinna Eldredge Cady.

Although Grandpa and Cady led rather different personal lives (the Cadys with no children or grandchildren to worry over, and Grandpa with so many to think of), they nevertheless shared enormous productivity in their mutual endeavors as writer and illustrator of the Burgess books and newspaper columns. They also shared the quiet fun of conversation, keen observation of the natural world, a congenial admiration and respect for each other, and an everlasting friendship, in which they always bestowed upon each other encouraging and moral support.

Cady introduced Grandpa to Moody B. Gates, the editor of the *People's Home Journal,* who also became a lifelong friend. Their meeting led to a monthly column called "The Green Meadow Club." Grandpa wrote stories that were both instructive about the natural world and entertaining. Cady provided the illustrations. Membership in the Green Meadow Club was open to any boy or girl who pledged to be kind to birds and animals and to protect them from their enemies. With each story the club offered prizes for the best letters from children about the animal or bird featured in the story. The Green Meadow Club was an immediate success and continued as such for twelve years.

Some little seeds of goodness
You'll find in every heart,
To sprout and keep on growing
When once they get a start.

During World War I, the club led a campaign to establish bird sanctuaries because of birds' value in controlling insect pests, thereby helping increase food production for the war effort. Grandpa's "Bedtime Stories," syndicated in many newspapers, capitalized on the idea and offered a button featuring Harrison Cady's Peter Rabbit and an engraved certificate of club membership. Two hundred thousand children joined the Green Meadow Club and offered their services to the wildlife sanctuaries. Nearly four thousand sanctuaries, encompassing over nine hundred thousand acres, were established in all parts of America through the efforts of this club.

Grandpa was recognized by the New York Zoological

Society in 1919 for his devotion to wildlife conservation. Dr. William T. Hornaday, director of the society, invited Grandpa and Nanna to the society's twenty-fifth annual meeting at the Waldorf Astoria. After the business part of the meeting, Grandpa was asked to come forward, and Dr. Hornaday presented him with the gold medal of the Wild Life Protection Fund for distinguished service to wildlife. Although taken a little by surprise, Grandpa was naturally very proud, as a writer of children's stories, to be accepted in the world of natural science. Dr. Hornaday remarked:

> In this busy and hurrying world occasionally a man is discovered who, like a Corliss engine, renders great service without making a loud noise. Often great things are accomplished quite unknown to those outside of the particular sphere of influence of the quiet worker. We have now to bring to your attention a case of that kind. I ask you to imagine a quiet and unassuming man, living in Springfield, Mass., who speaks daily, through the medium of about fifty newspapers, to an audience of more than 5,000,000 boys, girls, and parents. I ask you to imagine the value of thoroughly sound precepts of kindness and protection to wildlife placed before that audience throughout the past six years, through the medium of 2,200 Bedtime Stories and thirty-four books for schoolchildren. Such is the splendid record of achievement of Mr. Thornton W. Burgess; and along with this record

must be noted the fact that from first to last Mr. Burgess has carefully and consistently preserved the rights and ideals of legitimate sport with the gun and rod.

Grandpa had established himself as a writer and conservationist. His was to become a household name.

Chapter Two

*I*N 1920 MY MOTHER married a handsome young man from North Carolina, Robert Kohloss. Grandpa and Nanna gave the bride and groom a beautiful wedding, with Grandpa proudly escorting Helen down the aisle. After a short honeymoon the couple moved to Fall River, Massachusetts.

Helen returned to Grandpa and Nanna after my older brother and her first child, Robert, was born. It had been a difficult birth, and the baby bore scars from the use of forceps. My mother and Robert lived with Nanna and Grandpa until they were well enough to return home to Fall River. The following year, in August 1922, when I was born, my mother once again came to stay with Nanna. In spite of all the disturbance, noise, and confusion, Grandpa and Nanna were glad to make their home a haven for us all. Nanna's son Chester, my uncle, also had married by this time, and the house was frequented by his family as well.

With the arrival of my mother's third baby, my sister Rosemary, Nanna purchased a house in Springfield for my parents. My father had lost most of his money in the stock market and was having a difficult time earning enough to support the family. Grandpa was generous and gave him money in hopes that it would bring him out of his slump.

But my parents' relationship suffered as a result of these financial troubles. My mother began to see an old friend of hers, Bill Bradford, and soon they fell in love. Grandpa and Nanna were concerned that Helen was neglecting her responsibility to her children, as her infatuation with Bill consumed all her attention. Bill was a wealthy man with an active social life, unlike the Thornton Burgesses, and whenever he was around them he always seemed uneasy, as if in a hurry to leave for more pressing engagements. Nevertheless, my mother was smitten. Even though pregnant with my sister Jean, my mother asked for a divorce from my father. I would see him only once more after their separation. After Jean was born, my mother left us children with Grandpa and Nanna and married Bill in London, where he had been sent to manage the Wico Electric Company.

It's what you do
for others,
Not what they do
for you,
That makes you
feel so happy
All through and
through and
through.

At this trying time, Dr. Alfred Gross, professor of ornithology at Bowdoin College, asked Grandpa to accompany him on what had become an annual expedition for the two—to Martha's Vineyard to observe the last living heath hens. Grandpa usually went with Dr. Gross, but at this time my brother Robert, who suffered from chronic ear infections, had to have a serious mastoid operation. Grandpa decided his place was at home.

While my mother and Bill lived a carefree life in London, they were also trying to find a suitable place for the whole family to live. They finally chose a large top-floor flat on East Heath Road in Hampstead, about thirty minutes northwest of downtown London. Daddy-Bill, as we called our stepfather, felt that he should be responsible for only half the upkeep of the household, and the rest—including schooling, clothes, nanny, travel, and anything else that came under the heading of financial support for Helen's children—would have to be Nanna's responsibility. Thus our grandmother became our guardian.

In the spring of 1924, Grandpa had bought a summer home in Hampden, Massachusetts, just east of Springfield. It was the oldest house in town, built in 1742, with eighteen acres of meadows and woods. Here he could live in surroundings similar to those of the animal characters he liked to write about, where "a noisy little brook tumbles out of the hills and chuckles past a little gray house." He called it Laughing Brook.

Grandpa had a great impact on his grandchildren's lives, exerting a strong, nurturing influence over all of us. He was patient, kind, and loving, and we adored him. His world was

No home is ever mean or poor Where love awaits you at the door.

the world in which I was most comfortable, although I'm not sure he knew this. Strangely, he seemed to feel as if he didn't deserve all the love he received from us or the accolades and praise he received from others.

When we were young he smoked a pipe, which he never seemed to be without; but somewhere along the way he stopped smoking, and his pipe lay cradled in the pipe dish on the table beside his chair. Verse was always ready to jump onto the page from his pen; this ode to his pipe is just one example:

> *LINES TO AN OLD PIPE*
> *This ancient friend, who oft the air*
> *Perfumed with incense rich and rare*
> *To inspirations' God beguile,*
> *That he might ideas drop the while,*
> *I part with as one more than dear;*
> *As one to whom it is most clear,*
> *Such debt of gratitude I owe*
> *From fragrant clouds above this bowl*
> *Full many a tale I've seen unroll,*
> *And often in their streamers seem*
> *To find the substance of a dream,*
> *'Tis fitting that to lie in state,*
> *No less, should be my old Pal's fate.*

Grandpa wore rimless glasses hooked over his ears, and on special occasions he sometimes wore a pince-nez. He carried a round leather change purse in his back trouser pocket, which he would bring out occasionally, separating the coins in the palm of his hand to find just the right one for each one of us. When he was dressed up, he always wore a bow tie, and often he wore plus fours (long knickers). He kept a gold watch in his vest pocket, with a gold chain attached to the watch fob in the other pocket. He would remove the watch from its pocket, snap it open to observe the time, and then close it with a sharp click and replace it. Around Laughing Brook, he usually dressed comfortably in open-necked shirts, baggy pants, and moccasins.

We thought one of the best things about him was the wen on top of his head, shaped rather like a hen's egg, as he laughingly described it. But to us it was special, because in all the world, no one but Grandpa had one like it. One day, to our dismay, he announced that he was taking the advice of his doctor and having the wen surgically removed. Sometimes he would by mistake hit it against a door frame, causing wretched pain.

We had a special swing at Laughing Brook, just like the one Grandpa's great-uncle Charles had given him as a boy. He cut a board and hung it with long ropes from the horizontal branch of the old oak tree at the bottom of the esker at the brook, so he could watch us, and we could look up the hill and wave to him. We would always race to see who could get there first, because the last had to be the first pusher. Often we let our little sister Jean get a head start. We used to recite

TWB with his son, Thornton W. Burgess III, about 1909

TWB's birthplace at 6 School Street in Sandwich

TWB at work, about 1920

TWB's mother, Caroline Frances Haywood Burgess

TWB with his "Lady," Fannie Burgess.

TWB with a chickadee perched on the end of his rifle.

TWB in his study on the hill at Laughing Brook

The main house at Laughing Brook

TWB's stepdaughter Helen helps him edit a story
at the house in Springfield

TWB (right) in Panama with friend Alfred Gross
and Gross's son Bill

Robert Louis Stevenson's poem "The Swing," as taught to us
by Grandpa, as we would swing higher and higher:

> *Oh, how I love to go up in the swing,*
> *Up in the air so blue,*
> *Oh, I do think it the cleverest thing*
> *Ever a child can do.*
> *Up in the air and over the wall*
> *'Til I can see so wide . . .*

Sometimes my brother Robert turned the seat round and
round until the ropes were so tightly entwined they could go
no further. Then he let go and we spun so fast while it
unwound, we screamed with fear and delight, and either felt
sick or fell off the seat when it stopped, laughing our heads off.

At times we took trips together. When we grandchildren
visited Sandwich one day in spring, Grandpa took us to one
of his favorite spots to show us where, as a boy, he had picked
flowers to sell, including the trailing arbutus. He told us,
"The trailing arbutus is America's own flower. It grows
nowhere else in the world." I remember we got down on our
hands and knees to sniff the incomparable perfume of its
blossoms amid the competing odors of pine needles and salt
spray. The blossoms were lovely, pink, and gleaming. He also
showed us where his aunt Arabella Eldred Burgess had lived
at 4 Water Street. He and she had shared a love of nature. He
had often played there and tried to catch a fish or two at the

bottom of the slope from her house to the old mill pond, now called Lake Shawme.

As children, we loved the dunes of Cape Cod, blown by the wind into great hills and valleys of soft white sand, like great waves of undulating seas, scattered with beach plum, scrub, and grasses. Two of my favorite places to take a picnic and spend the day in summer were the dunes of Sandwich and those of Barney's Joy in South Dartmouth on Buzzards Bay. My family had a key to unlock the private gate at Barney's, where the local farmers took their cows there to graze just as they had in Sandwich years before. As we drove down the winding dirt road towards the sea, we would pass ribbons of pink marsh mallows on either side, with scrub and grassy meadowland and salt marshes as far as the eye could see, freshwater ponds here and there, and the sound of the sea in the distance.

When we reached the sea, I gazed skyward at the gulls, the terns, and once in a while what appeared to be a giant sandpiper I called Yellow Legs. I watched the little sandpipers fly in flocks along the white sandy beaches. They turned in the air in unison so exactly that they looked like a corps de ballet. They would then alight all at once, scurrying this way and that along the edge of the sea. Then down would go their slender bills into the wet sand as they searched for the small living things washed up by the waves.

Grandpa would wander the shoreline, taking visual notes and picking up a shell now and then. Soon he would traipse along the salt marshes, and I would follow. With surprise and pleasure he would pass on his observations, instilling in me that same feeling of awe at every new discovery.

Later, when he wrote *The Burgess Seashore Book for Children,* he dedicated it to us four grandchildren, Robert, Frances, Rosemary, and Jean—in recognition, I think, for all the fun and enthusiasm we had shared together by the seashore.

And so my grandparents' house became "home" in the hearts of their grandchildren. As time passed, my brother and sisters and I attended many different boarding schools, but every time we felt lonely, we asked to go to Grandpa and Nanna's house, where we felt loved and welcomed.

Home, no matter where it be, Or it be big or small, Is just the one place in the world That dearest is of all.

Tragically, Grandpa never had as close a relationship with his own son, Thornton III. I realized as I grew older how much this loss haunted him. Young Thornton never understood nor appreciated Grandpa's way of being moved by the beauty of the sky or the hills, the glimmer of the sun on water, or any other phenomena of nature. The safety, love, and warmth that my siblings and I shared with my grandparents was lost on Grandpa's only son.

Holidays with my grandparents on Washington Road in Springfield always involved huge meals that took a long time to prepare. Mealtimes would be full of chatter and laughing, hopping up and down, setting and clearing the table, eating and spilling food. For Christmas we decked the house with holly and mistletoe, put wreaths on the front and back doors, and decorated our fragrant balsam Christmas tree, on which Grandpa would always place, as the very last thing, the gold star of Bethlehem. Nanna would use her best table linens, her family silver, her cranberry-colored Sandwich glass goblets, and her Royal Worcester china for the Christmas table setting. In the center of the table she would arrange Christmas greens with silver candlesticks on either side and dishes of nuts to crack at either end.

The day before Christmas, Grandpa would hand the milkman, the mailman, the newspaper boy, and the iceman their Christmas envelopes. He made sure he greeted each one personally to wish him a happy holiday.

Anticipation of Christmas morning was almost too much for us children, but at last it arrived amid much joyous screaming and laughter. When the stockings had been emptied, the fire was lit in the fireplace. As the logs flamed and crackled, the presents were opened, with paper and ribbons scattering everywhere. When all was done, we girls would put on our new Christmas dresses (usually alike) and the boys their new shirts and ties. Grandpa wore a bright red bow tie and tried out his new pipe.

Soon dinner was served: roast beef, Yorkshire pudding, mashed potatoes and dark gravy, assorted vegetables and

Brussels sprouts (one of Grandpa's favorites, but only popular with most of us the next day when they were combined with left-over mashed potatoes to make "bubble and squeak"). For dessert we had homemade pies, ice cream, and rich dark plum pudding made with suet, raisins, currants, citron, brown sugar, eggs, cream, and brandy. Grandpa poured warmed cognac over the top of the pudding and then held a lit match to it. We all held our breath as it suddenly burst into a beautiful blue flame. When the flame went down, Grandpa gave Nanna and other adults a small portion with a spoonful of brandy butter and then helped himself to rather large portions of both. He would smile at us and say, "My dears, I know this is not to your taste now, but some day you will know what you are missing." And of course we did. Christmas was the only occasion I can remember on which liquor or wine was served in that house.

After dinner, as it was still early, we continued in the holiday spirit, singing carols and dancing to Nanna's twanging Jew's harp. She held the small lyre-shaped instrument between her teeth and plucked the metal piece with her finger, swaying to the rhythm of the tune. How clever and pretty and fun we thought she was. Grandpa had never learned to dance and could not carry a tune, but he would sit in his chair pretending to read, peeking over the top of the newspaper with a twinkle in his appreciative glance.

People were always coming by the house to see Grandpa. Natural scientists beat paths to his door in Springfield and (in summers) in Hampden after he had become a successful writer. Others visited his birthplace in Sandwich. Some—like the writer for the *Boston Evening Transcript*, who arrived at the Springfield house in August 1926—were surprised by what they found:

> *One Saturday under a Mediterranean-blue sky I tracked Thornton Burgess to his lair, and it was a blow not to find something about the Burgess residence that would tell the world that here lived the man who controls the destinies of whole generations of wild folk, who feeds daily the insatiable minds of approximately five million children. The home is but a roomy white comfortable-looking place with back yard just large enough to accommodate the house. There was no evidence of a menagerie. We had planned to see cages of jays, sparrows, chickadees, not to mention skunk farms, fox farms and bunny farms, all nicely labeled Sammy Jay, White Throat, Tommy Tit, Jimmy Skunk, Reddy Fox, and Peter Rabbit. Well, it was a little bit like opening the doctor's bag on a stork's visit, and finding nothing in it—no baby. Mr. Burgess even denied often visiting the zoo in his neighborhood.*
>
> *"What can you tell about animals when they are in a state of captivity?" he exclaimed.*

To us children it seemed that everyone knew him. He used to receive letters addressed to "Peter Rabbit, Somewhere in the United States" or "Laughing Brook, USA," or simply "Peter Rabbit's grandfather." People stopped by his house with injured animals, asking for help. We grew accustomed to a steady stream of visitors bearing raccoons, snakes, muskrat, rabbits, and skunks. Grandpa did the best he could with some and took others, like birds with badly broken wings and animals caught in steel leg traps, to a veterinary hospital.

When he felt like getting away, he often would drive us in his large Packard touring car on sightseeing trips through the Berkshire hills, stopping along the way to point out aspects of the remarkable views. The sharp, narrow turns and roller-coaster hills were always scary and exciting.

Sometimes he would take one or all to the lectures he gave at schools, science museums, clubs, and universities. He received so many invitations to speak, he couldn't possibly accept them all. He was also asked to tell some of his stories for children over the radio and to give a talk afterward about birds and animals. This enterprise turned out to be a great success, and in 1924 the Radio Nature League was born. Its purpose was to conserve America's wildlife and scenic wonders. As his listening audience grew, Grandpa was nearly overcome by telephone calls and correspondence from fans.

Every day is different from every other day, And always there is something new along the way.

All this he did without remuneration of any kind, as there were few paying programs in those early years of radio.

Through the cooperation of the Boston Museum of Natural History, the predecessor of the Boston Museum of Science, the Radio Nature League presented talks by noted ornithologists. One of these was Grandpa's good friend and colleague Dr. Alfred O. Gross, the ornithologist who was a professor at Bowdoin College. Dr. Gross was studying the diseases and parasites of the ruffed grouse in an effort to understand its alarming decrease in numbers in the eastern states. Dr. Gross's study required specimens, so Grandpa explained on the air what Dr. Gross was doing. He asked listeners to send any dead grouse they found to Dr. Gross, and he asked hunters to aid the investigation by sending him the intestines of birds they had shot. The Radio Nature League proved to be the most important source of data for this study, contributing some two thousand specimens and creating an international interest in the preservation of this beautiful bird.

Sometimes Grandpa, at the request of Dr. Gross, had injured birds sent to him from "bird hospitals" for his close observation.

September 25, 1929

Dear Alfred:

I was glad to get your letter today and know that you had received the other two birds. The one with the injured wing Miss Coburn has had but a short time. The other one, as I wrote you before, has been boss of the Bird Hospital for nearly a year. I had intended to get some motion pictures of this bird before it was sent, but when Miss Coburn telephoned me of the opportunity to send the birds up, I told her to go ahead by all means.

You said something to me about wanting some data on that nighthawk. I have forgotten just what you wanted, but here is the story. The bird was found roosting on a pile of wood back of Forest Park the morning of September 12. The City Forester telephoned me and I went over with the camera. I found that I could approach until the lens of my camera was within three feet without arousing a protest. Nearer than that the bird got uneasy. I noted that the right wing dropped. Evidently it had been injured. When I undertook to put my hand on the bird, it flew, but almost immediately settled on another log a short distance away. There I dropped a hat over it and brought the bird home. It is now at the Bird Hospital and thriving. Beneath the right wing is a bunch. This Miss Coburn is reducing with Absorbine, Jr. The bird eats well and is very fond of milk. It knows the difference between whole milk and skim milk and will have none of the latter. It flies about the rooms. There's the story on the nighthawk. . . .

Faithfully yours,

Thornton

Because of his talks on the air, Grandpa was always receiving birds, animals, insects, and reptiles, dead or alive, to identify and comment upon. Some incidents were not without humor. One evening a package that had come by parcel post awaited him when he arrived at the radio studio. It was about the size of a two-pound candy box and tied securely with string; the cover was perforated with pinholes. He opened the box to find nothing there. But from the bottom of the box, along the outside wrapper, a pretty little head appeared with bright staring eyes that never blinked, while a delicate forked tongue darted out and in. It was a little milk snake about eighteen inches long, with the circumference of a slender pencil; a more harmless little creature could not be found.

But regardless of size, a snake is a snake. No one in the studio would touch it. Only five minutes were left before Grandpa was due to go on the air. It would have been useless to put the snake back in the box in which it had arrived. So the announcer, Gordon Swan, got another box into which Grandpa tucked the little reptile, tying up the box tightly.

Grandpa had been on the air for about five minutes when he chanced to glance at the engineer, who was getting to his feet. Taking off his earphones, the engineer tiptoed toward Grandpa, pointing downward at his table. He couldn't speak, because the microphone was open. Grandpa looked where he pointed. Gliding across the table was the little snake, although the box appeared to be tied just as Grandpa had left it. Grandpa asked his listeners to excuse him for a moment, as there was a snake loose in the studio and he must catch it. Having picked the little reptile up, he told his audience he was holding the snake while he finished his talk. He knew that most of those listening undoubtedly saw, in their imagination, a five- or six-foot reptile, so he did not disabuse them of this notion. Since none of us children was afraid of snakes, at least not the little snakes we found around Laughing Brook, we thought this story hilarious.

Grandpa used to laugh when he thought of the alacrity with which the announcer, Gordon Swan, fled the studio the time Grandpa put a live rattlesnake on the air. This program was meant to promote safety education. He had heard of a teenage boy who, bare-handed, had caught a four-foot rattler. He arranged for the boy to bring the reptile to the studio so listeners could hear the sound a rattler makes. A herpetologist friend used a snake hook to guide the rattler to coil in front of the microphone. Swan waited outside the studio, watching through an observation window until preparations were complete. At the last minute he hurried in and almost stuttered in his haste to introduce the program and get out of the studio again. The snake did his part, and his whirring rattle over the air waves brought many letters of thanks from listeners who felt better for knowing what it sounded like.

One evening in late winter, Grandpa devoted his radio talk to enhancing roadside beauty by controlling the tent caterpillar. He taught his audience what the caterpillar's egg clusters looked like and where to find them, hoping that listeners would help destroy them. He explained that the eggs were deposited in small clusters on the twigs of the caterpillar's favorite trees. Each cluster was encased in a varnish-like covering that hardened. Throughout winter, when the trees are bare, these clusters are easy to find. In the early spring, simultaneous with the bursting of the brown leaf buds, the caterpillar eggs hatch. With the birth of the delicate green leaves, the work of defoliation begins. The tiny worms at once begin spinning their silken communal tents, where they spend the cool nights and seek shelter in bad weather. When the caterpillars are fully grown they are about two inches long. By this time a large branch of a big tree or all of a small tree may be completely stripped of leaves.

Grandpa announced that in March there would be a contest for boys and girls of high school age, with prizes for the student who collected the most egg clusters. The egg clusters were to be delivered to a schoolteacher or group leader, who would then count and burn them, reporting the totals to Grandpa.

The first campaign was such a success that it became an annual event. The Massachusetts Department of Agriculture offered cups and other prizes for Bay State girls and boys with the highest totals, and other states followed suit. Whole towns were virtually cleared of the pest that for years had detracted from the good appearance of their roadsides. One boy, working alone in the Boston parks, collected over forty-five thousand clusters, a great service to his community and to all who made use of the parks.

As children, Robert, Rosemary, and I were featured on the Radio Nature League with Grandpa once. The studio was in the once quite elegant Hotel Kimball. We each had a little script. I remember that the three of us were very shy. We certainly weren't actors, so I think we probably sounded timid. But the experience was still exciting. I never heard what I actually sounded like, and it was hard to imagine that thousands of other people did.

Grandpa educated adults as well as children. From reading his books, one can learn a tremendous amount about the ways of a particular animal and its habitat. When I've forgotten something about Jerry Muskrat or any other furred or feathered creature, I pick up Grandpa's story about him and learn all over again. Although some think that his books are just for children, I find them rewarding for all ages. Others agree with me; for example, Grandpa once received the following letter from Texas about Johnny Chuck's adventures:

> *Please do rescue little Chuck soon. There are two of us children who cannot stand the strain of waiting much longer for his rescue. We sit down every evening before we go to bed, and the older child reads to the younger and both enjoy your little stories on the woods and fields. But please remember that folk in their first and second child-*

hood should not have their emotions kept at high tension very long. So hasten to rescue little Chuck and relieve the heart strain of

> *One child, age 7 years*
> *One child, age 70 years.*

Federal judge Harold Medina confirmed that Grandpa's writings had played an important role in his adult life. As Hawthorne Daniel's biography of the famous jurist notes,

> *There were few light moments during the long and stressful trial of the Rosenbergs [a Communist couple indicted for treason], but each morning, during the short recess the judge regularly ordered, an amusing little program was reenacted. Leaving the courtroom and going to the judge's room adjacent to it, Medina chose a comfortable chair and opened the morning edition of the* New York Herald Tribune. *Headlines almost always referred to the case that was before him. Not infrequently editorials did the same, and cartoons now and again touched upon the subject.*
>
> *But none of these caught his attention during those midmorning recesses. Instead he opened the paper to the pages on which the Thornton W. Burgess Nature Stories appeared, and carefully read of the adventures of Peter Rabbit and Reddy Fox, or Grandfather Frog and Jimmy Skunk, of Sammy Jay and Old Mother Nature, and Buster Bear and the rest.*

Not a day passed without the morning recess and not a morning recess passed without a Thornton Burgess story. Here was real help for a tired and troubled judge— clean and simple little stories for little children to bring relief of the constant pressure of the courtroom.

In his career as a writer, Grandpa never thought of making a lot of money. He just wanted to teach people about what was important to him, the science of natural history. In an article for *Natural History* (volume XXII, number 2), the official magazine of the American Museum of Natural History in New York City, he wrote:

Nature was the first teacher of the human race. With this statement no one can take issue. It was not until our prehistoric ancestors began to observe the workings of nature and tried to discover the law governing the manifestations which they observed, that they began to rise above the animals surrounding them. Every upward step since is traceable directly to increased knowledge of the laws governing life, and these laws are the laws of Nature and have existed from the beginning. Nature was the first teacher and still is the universal teacher.

This being true, it seems to me a fatal defect in our present educational systems that nature study is given so small a part. In the curriculum of the average public school, nature study has such a minor place that it becomes almost negligible. Yet it should be the foundation on which the educational system is based. In the study of Nature lies the key to the most successful mental, moral, and spiritual development of the child. I question if there is another subject which can even approach animal life in universal appeal to young and old.

In his autobiography Grandpa explained further the value of nature education and nature stories:

When I began writing animal stories for children, it was with the sole purpose of teaching the facts about the forms of animal life most familiar to American children. I endeavored to do this by stimulating the imagination, which is the birthright of every child, at the same time holding absolutely to the truth so far as the facts concerning the subject of each story were concerned. No child will admit that any animal knows more than he does, and this is especially true in regard to smaller animals. This attitude has been singularly illustrated in the matter of moral lessons. A story containing an obvious moral and centering around human characters immediately becomes personal. There is instant recognition that that moral is intended for the reader, and is resented.

On the other hand an animal story may have a moral introduced in the very beginning without giving the slight-

est offense. The psychology of it is that those morals are pointed at the animal characters and not at the children. The latter not only do not resent those morals but heartily approve of them. If Peter Rabbit has done that which is wrong or foolish, they desire that he should be taught his lesson. Unconsciously they absorb these morals themselves.

In all the stories Grandpa wrote of the natural world, he never allowed any of his characters to be killed. An editorial writer for a Maine paper once poked fun at this Pollyanna-like attitude, asking, "When does Mr. Coyote eat?"

Grandpa replied, "Tragedy comes into the lives of children soon enough. There's no reason to hasten it."

Yet in our family life, Grandpa would gently introduce us to such aspects of nature, doing so with both kindness and candor. When my grandfather told me of the great whale he had seen flensed by the whalemen during his childhood, the story had quite an effect on me. I always prayed that the other harpooned whale had recovered and made its way home to the deep ocean, never to be captured again. When I first heard the story of the whales, I jumped into the safety of Grandpa's lap and, with my arms around his neck, said, "Know what, Grandpa? I love you." Perhaps it was a way to reassure him, and myself, that we could support each other when facing the inexplicably harsh and cruel aspects of life.

Chapter Three

ONE OF THE MOST unforgettable characters Grandpa ever met was Alice Rebecca Cooke of Sandwich, whom everyone called Aunt Sally. She ran what she called the Woodhouse Night Club in the woodshed that opened off her kitchen. There she nightly entertained skunks and raccoons who would come and go through the cat hole. They were so friendly and unafraid that they unhesitatingly climbed into her lap to drink milk from the pan she held. Miss Cooke allowed Grandpa to take motion pictures of these scenes, and he often sat with her, camera at the ready, from dusk to dawn.

Aunt Sally was scrupulously neat. Every morning she picked up and burned the newspapers with which she had covered the floor of the woodshed the night before. The food pans were washed and scalded, and then the banquet for the coming night was prepared, which included many loaves of bread from the local bakery. At various times she hosted as many as fifteen skunks or eighteen raccoons.

Miss Cooke comfortably seated herself in a low chair, beside which she arranged three boxes as steps leading up to her lap. Often two or three animals would sit in her lap at the same time, drinking out of the same pan. The night I was there, a skunk and a raccoon together crawled into Aunt Sally's lap and drank peacefully together. Grandpa and Nanna also took turns occupying Aunt Sally's chair. Once I myself had the thrill of sitting in it, and two skunks crept up to my lap and drank milk from the pan.

There came a time when this dear old lady could no longer entertain her guests, so she had to close the cat hole into the night club. But one day she heard a scratching on the screen door and found a woodchuck looking up at her. Aunt Sally invited her into the kitchen, and by

Nothing that you ever do,
Nothing good or nothing bad,
But has effect on other folks—
Gives them pain or makes them glad.

using the empty boxes, Aunt Sally arranged steps to the tabletop, where the two breakfasted together. On Aunt Sally's ninetieth birthday I was privileged, with Grandpa, Nanna, Gordon Swan, and others, to share a piece of the birthday cake with the woodchuck and Aunt Sally at the table. The animal would eat anything—bread, cookies, pie, candied fruit, doughnuts—and was totally unabashed at the number of admirers visiting that day. Grandpa always used his lantern slides of Aunt Sally and her animal guests for his lectures about her, and they were a huge success.

Watching and recording, essentials of the nature writer's craft, were constant activities for Grandpa all his life. In 1927, under the auspices of the National Research Council in Washington, he went on an expedition to Panama with his friend Dr. Gross to study birds of the jungle. Nanna, my brother Robert and I, and Dr. Gross's wife and their three children accompanied them. While the others stayed at a hotel in Balboa, fourteen-year-old Bill Gross (a budding naturalist) accompanied his father and Grandpa on the early-morning train for Frijoles, midway along the Panama Canal on the shore of Gatun Lake, the largest artificial lake in the world. Created by the damming of the Chagres River, Gatun Lake provides the flow of water needed for working the locks of the canal.

By staying here and sitting still, I'm sure I'll simply grow quite ill. A change of scene is what I need To be from all my troubles freed.

At Frijoles, the threesome took a launch for Barro Colorado Island, the largest island in the lake. The island had been created at the time of the original flooding of the canal, and its various species of animal and bird life had been forced to higher ground as the water gradually rose. This created an unusual concentration of tropical wildlife in the unsubmerged areas that formed the island. This paradise had been set aside as an institute for tropical research by the Canal Zone government. A laboratory with modern facilities had been built so that scientists could observe animal and plant life under almost ideal conditions.

The course to the island was marked by buoys to help launches avoid the submerged trees. Occasionally my grandfather and his friends passed a stump or dead tree on which beautiful orchids had found footholds. To either side of the lake they could see banana plantations and native thatched huts. As they approached a deep cove, they could see the buildings of the Laboratory for Tropical Research, where they would make their headquarters for the next three weeks. Save for the little clearing immediately around the laboratory, the entire island was virgin jungle.

Grandpa would later tell one of his radio audiences,

As we started up the long climb of 199 steps (I don't know why they didn't make it 200) leading to the laboratory, the most gorgeous butterfly I have ever seen—the upper surface of its wings a brilliant metallic blue—flitted back and forth, now into the darkness of the jungle, now out in the open. High overhead circled a white hawk with black-banded wings and tail—the black and white hawk of Panama. It was the size of our familiar red-tail. I saw this hawk and his mate almost every day while I was there. Overhead the tropical sun poured down, and by the time we had reached the last of those 199 steps, I at least was as wet as if I had jumped overboard into the lake.

Grandpa reveled in the opportunity to study new and exotic animal and plant life, and in his diary he recorded his first sightings of creatures that were unusual to him, such as sloths, anteaters, king vultures, lizards, and butterflies of all kinds, of which he took many photographs. When Grandpa returned after three weeks to the hotel where Nanna, Robert, and I had been staying, Robert—who was recovering from a long hospital stay following his mastoid operation—showed Grandpa how he had gone swimming in the hotel pool each day, gaining more strength until he could swim the whole width. To celebrate this achievement, Grandpa pulled his round leather change purse out of his back pocket and gave Robert a silver dollar.

Grandpa, Robert, and I spent much time together. We often banded birds so that naturalists and bird enthusiasts could follow their habits of migration and their numbers. We set up simple traps, with a stick holding up one opening, and then placed some seeds inside. After tying a string to the stick, we ran the string through the window and waited indoors, where we had a good view. Robert and I watched, and whenever birds alighted we pulled the string, temporarily trapping them. Then we banded them, replacing old bands, when we found them, with new useful information. When with my hand I gently cradled the birds on their backs, they remained perfectly still, making it easy to band them. The moment I turned them over, they instantly flew away.

In the spring of 1927, while my mother Helen and stepfather
Bill were in London, Nanna became ill with pneumonia.
Grandpa did not change his clothes for three days and
three nights while he sat by her side, holding her
hand and crying now and then. My sisters and
brother and I were sent to stay with nearby
relatives and friends, and Grandpa wrote
to our mother, telling her she must come
to look after us as soon as she could
secure passage from England. Helen
soon arrived, and Grandpa met her at
the dock in New York. She discharged
Nanna's nurse and stayed with her, caring
for her mother herself until she recovered.
Grandpa and Nanna were both grateful to have Helen
home again, for they had missed her.

*The hurts that hardest
are to bear
Come from those for
whom we care.*

Once Nanna recovered, my mother arranged to take us all
back to London with her, but I developed a case of mumps
one week before we were to sail. My sister Rosemary had to be
quarantined, but Robert, who had already had the mumps,
and Jean, who was just a baby, were allowed to sail with Helen
while Rosemary and I stayed with Nanna and Grandpa
another month until we had recovered.

Just before Christmas of 1927, Grandpa received a letter
from his son, Thornton, who had moved back from
California to live outside Boston. His son wrote that he had
fallen in love with a young woman named Mildred Peterson,

and they were engaged to be married on January 14, 1928, which happened to be Grandpa's fifty-fourth birthday. Grandpa wrote to Thornton and to his fiancée that he did not think Thornton was prepared financially or otherwise to undertake such a step at this time. Could they not wait? He received a reply from Mildred saying they were going ahead with the wedding, soon followed by a note from Thornton describing their plans—in which Grandpa was not asked to take part. Neither he nor Nanna was invited to the wedding. Once more disappointment over his strained relationship with his son weighed heavily upon him.

On the day of his son's wedding, Grandpa went with Nanna to New York City to visit with Harrison and Melinna Cady at their home. Nanna knew that Harrison would cheer Grandpa with his whimsical and infectious humor, as he always did. They rambled on about their similar childhood experiences and struggles. Then Harrison brought Grandpa up to date on one of his yarns, saying, "Have I told you about my latest bustle?" With the usual twinkle in his eyes, he went on, "I acquired a new bustle just the other day. This one's another good one. It belonged to Marie Grosholtz, better known as Madame Tussaud." Grandpa chuckled in anticipation of Cady's explanation of how he acquired it—told at great length and full of his inimitable humor.

Before Grandpa and Nanna left, Cady said with his eyes still twinkling, "There is a local woman in Rockport [the coastal Massachusetts town where the Cadys spent their summers] who was told that shredded cigars scattered among her roses would protect them from rabbits. She did this," he said, "and one night as Melinna and I were coming home, we saw a great cloud of smoke rising from her property. We rushed over, and what did we see, but forty little rabbits sitting on the wall, all smoking freshly rolled cigars."

Grandpa and Nanna returned to their hotel, feeling a renewed sense of well-being. Melinna and Harrison were their dearest friends and confidants, and their business and social relationship grew stronger with the years.

We all loved seeing the Cadys when they came to visit. One day when Cady was with Grandpa in Springfield, he remarked, "You know, Thornton, you should start a real collection of these lovely little bottles you have found over the years." Grandpa had always treasured his few shiny odd-shaped green and brown bottles, so he decided to look for more. A collection of these hand-blown translucent bottles of every size and shape soon filled his sunroom on Washington Road, and he marveled at their myriad of lights—mellow browns, blues, and greens.

To long for home when far away Will rob of joy the brightest day.

By the spring of 1929, the four of us children were living in Hampstead, England, with Helen and Bill. Rosemary and I were enrolled in Frognal Country Day School, while Robert went to Upland House, a boarding school in Surrey from which he came home only on holiday.

We exchanged lots of letters and packages across the sea with our grandparents, whom we sorely missed.

Dear Nanna and Grandpa,

Thank you for your letters. I am sorry I take so long to write. Everybody misses you a lot and wishes you were here.

We like our flat. It is right on the Heath where there are lots of ponds full of ducks and geese and swans, and there are lots of trees and paths so we play hide and seek. . . . We have some new friends who live near us. Robert's best friend is Peter Dgkelly who is a Russian Prince. He and his sister Tamara, and their mother escaped from Russia so they wouldn't get killed in the revolution. Rosemary and I walk to Frognal Country Day School every day, but it is so foggy we have to hold hands because we can hardly see each other. It is very cold at school. I turned blue the first day so Mummy had to fetch me and take me home. She put me in bed with lots of blankets and hot tea to get me warm.

Our Nanny is very nice. She is fat, and laughs and hugs us a lot. She stays home with Jean when we leave for school after she makes sure we've finished our breakfast, had our spoonful of black syrupy tonic (which we hate), and dressed properly in our navy serge uniforms, hats, coats, and leggings and mittens. We like Elsa our cook too. She has pretty red hair and sometimes cooks us kippers for breakfast. I like kippers as much as you, Grandpa, but nobody else does much. When we come home from school she makes us cambric tea, scones with butter and strawberry jam. It's yummy. On Sundays we eat in the dining room with Mummy and Daddy-Bill, but we are not allowed to speak at the table. If we say something bad or spill something by mistake, we are sent back to the kitchen, and sometimes to our room. Jean makes the most mistakes because she's too young to understand.

I hope all the snow is gone at your house by now, Grandpa, so you don't have to shovel so much, and the ice is melting at Laughing Brook so you can go there soon. We have not had any snow here, just cold rain and fog. But we've gotten used to it.

Lots and lots of love from Frances

Nanna and Grandpa wrote us many letters in return, and these were eagerly awaited and treasured. Grandpa told us that sometimes the snow was piled so high in the long driveway at Washington Road that it took him all morning to clear it. During the winter months, he went down to check on Laughing Brook, particularly after heavy snow and wind storms, to make sure no damage had occurred.

In late winter and very early spring he described how

Laughing Brook was changing; in January and February the trees, meadows, and ice along the edge of the brook were covered with snow. The still water under the road bridge was frozen. The frogs remained buried for the winter under the mud, waiting for spring at the bottom of the Smiling Pool, which was smothered with ice and snow. Jerry Muskrat, who could feed under the ice, could be seen only if one waited patiently for him to briefly appear before returning to his house underwater, where he was always warm. In late March the trees and fields were still and bare, and the purple hills seemed painted on the landscape in the distance. By April and May, the trees and grasses were bending and swaying, green once more. Soon signs of rebirth appeared everywhere, and Grandpa wrote of them with joy in his letters, looking forward to his summer return to Laughing Brook.

In England during summers (except for the two during which we happily returned to Laughing Brook) my mother rented a cottage in Bognor on the south coast, east of Portsmouth. Every day our nanny, our beloved "old nurse" who would leave us only after she was married, took us children to the beach. We built sand castles and buried each other up to the neck, splashed and swam, caught crabs, and played tricks to scare Nanny.

During the summer of 1930, Nanna and Grandpa came to visit us at Bognor and Hampstead. It was the best summer we ever had there. At Bognor we built sand castles and moats and then watched them cave in under the incoming tide. Although we played and swam as children do at the beach, we now had Grandpa close by to tell us marvelous stories of the wonders of the seashore.

One day, after a storm had passed, we discovered masses of jellyfish along the sand.
Some were swimming in shallow water and
looked like umbrellas, their delicate, wavy
edges set with threads that pulsated in the
water. We knew better than to touch
them, as I had once been stung, and
once was enough. As we watched these
milky discs on the sand, they mysteriously
disappeared, leaving only wet circles.

Look not too much on that behind
Lest to the future you be blind.

"What happened? Where did they go?" we asked Grandpa. With his usual chuckle, he told us that jellyfish are made up mostly of water, and when stranded on the beach under the hot sun, they simply disintegrate. At night, Grandpa took me down to the water's edge to show me the phosphorescent lights made by the jellyfish after the storm. He said, "They make the water look as if it is on fire." I told him the lights looked like fairies dancing on the surface of the sea, sparkling and beautiful.

Back in Hampstead with our parents and grandparents, we played on the heath. Our old nurse took us to London sometimes to watch the changing of the guard at Buckingham Palace. Twice we went to Kensington Gardens and, by chance, played with Princess Margaret and Princess Elizabeth when they were there with their nanny. We avidly read about A. A. Milne's Christopher Robin and Winnie the Pooh, and never stepped on the lines in the sidewalk—we knew it was bad luck because of the bears "who wait at the corner to eat/the sillies who tread on the lines in the street." We relayed this information to Grandpa and Nanna and warned them to avoid stepping on the lines when we took them to see the changing of the guard and to visit Madame Tussaud's wax museum. We rode with them on top of double-decker buses to tour London, something we never did with our parents.

After Nanna and Grandpa returned to the United States, he wrote the following advice in a letter to Harrison Cady, showing that he enjoyed discovering the delights of the city as much as those of the country:

May 7, 1931

When you are in London, call Helen up if you have a chance. It will do her good just to hear your voice. . . .

You will want to eat at the Cheshire Cheese; also Ye Old Cock Tavern on Fleet St. The latter was a favorite with Dickens. You probably will eat at Simpson's on the Strand, which is famous for its roast beef, but is a modern place. One of the most interesting eating places is Simpson's Fish Ordinary on Bird-in-Hand Court, Cheapside. You will get soup, three courses of fish, crack-

*ers and cheese and a lot of quaint ceremony and atmos-
phere. . . . This lunch with its attendant ceremony of cut-
ting the cheese and guessing its weight has been
continuous for 200 years.*

One summer, Grandpa wrote us about a surprise he had
encountered one night while reading in his rocking chair, as
was his habit at Laughing Brook before going to bed at about
eleven o'clock—always the last one to turn in. While quietly
sitting there, he thought he heard a knocking at the old
kitchen door. He listened for a moment or two and, hearing
nothing more, continued to read. Soon he heard a distinct
knock. He got up and opened the door to see who could possibly be there at that hour. He looked out into the darkness but
saw no one. A bit bewildered, he closed the door and returned
to his chair. Just as he picked up his book, he heard another
very distinct, even louder knock on the door. This time he
walked quickly, turned the outside light on, opened the door,
and looking down, saw to his great surprise Jimmy Skunk,
with a rather large, clear glass bottle stuck on his head.

"So this is who you are," he exclaimed to himself. "What
a strange predicament you've got yourself into, young fellow,"
he said softly so as not to frighten Jimmy. "You had better
come in with me 'til I can think of some way to get that dang
thing off."

He picked up Jimmy and carried him into the kitchen,
where he looked for a blunt instrument with which to break

the glass. He found a knife with a large handle and wrapped the sharp end in a kitchen towel. Then he gently put Jimmy down on the counter, placed the bottle over the sink, and gave it a sharp whack with the knife handle. The bottle broke clean. Not a splinter penetrated Jimmy's head or neck, and he was free—all this without once giving a sign of wanting to perfume the air. Grandpa then picked Jimmy up gently in his arms and said, "There's a brave young fellow." He deposited him outside the old kitchen door. Jimmy turned as if to say thank-you and then, with his usual slow, waddling gait, disappeared into the darkness. I always wondered how Jimmy Skunk had known where to turn in his plight.

On each of our three Christmases in England (we spent two back home in Springfield with Grandpa and Nanna), Grandpa arranged to have our mother phone his house at one o'clock Greenwich Mean Time, which was eight o'clock in the morning in Springfield—just after we had emptied our stockings and opened our presents. He wanted to surprise Nanna, who felt bereft whenever we were not home for the holidays. Promptly at eight o'clock the phone would ring, and we all had a chance to wish each other a merry Christmas.

Thank-you letters were sent and received for all the wonderful gifts exchanged, and Grandpa often thanked us in poems, like this one sent to Robert after the Christmas of 1929:

I light my pipe and sit me down
To take my ease and dream
Of loved ones in a distant land
Until at last they seem
Not off beyond the rolling waves,
Not far across the sea,
But truly in my presence here
And very close to me.
The smoke curls up above the bowl
And for a little space
There's naught but just a pleasant haze
And then I see a face.
'Tis of a laddie that I love,
His features all aglow
With laughter in his merry eyes
And love for me I know.
I hear his laugh, I feel his cheek
Close pressed against my own;
I hold him tight and for a time
I am no more alone.
Oh Laddie 'tis a magic pipe
You sent across the sea
For when I sit me down to smoke
It brings you close to me.

Grandpa and his friend Dr. Gross conducted an annual census of the heath hen population on Martha's Vineyard, where the last of the birds made their home. They photographed the birds from a blind set up at the farm of James Green, located on the state highway between Edgartown and West Tisbury. In colonial times the heath hen had been abundant from Maine to the Carolinas. But the birds' habit of congregating in open fields, where they made an easy target, contributed to their decline.

By 1870 the heath hen had been entirely exterminated on the mainland and could be found only in its last stronghold, Martha's Vineyard. The state of Massachusetts established a reservation on the Vineyard in an attempt to increase the heath hens' numbers. The birds increased from less than one hundred to an estimated two thousand in 1916. Unfortunately, a fire swept over the entire breeding area that May, and the following year less than one hundred and fifty birds remained. The heath hen was very susceptible to poultry diseases, and when domestic turkeys were introduced to the Vineyard in large numbers, a disease called blackhead came with them. In 1920 many birds were found dead or in a weak and helpless condition. The 1927 spring census showed only thirteen heath hens. By 1928 the flock had dwindled to three males. During the fall of 1928 only two birds were seen, and after December 8, but one was reported.

In the springtime of earlier years, the heath hen had appeared in the open fields in the early morning hours and again in the late afternoon, demonstrating its extraordinary courtship ritual. The male inflated his curious orange sacs and made a loud, rolling, hollow call not unlike the sound made by blowing hard over the open neck of a heavy bottle and somewhat like the mating call of the prairie chicken, called booming. It can only be imagined today.

In his autobiography, Grandpa wrote about the spring of 1931, when he watched the last heath hen search for a mate:

> It was sheer, stark tragedy. Watching that lone bird displaying all his charms, calling for a mate after the manner of his race down through thousands of years, and while I knew that nowhere in all the world was there a mate or even a companion for him, that I was watching the very end of one of Nature's creative experiments down through the ages, bathed with infinite pathos a scene that should have been fascinating and delightful. A form of wild life had failed utterly in adaptation to changed conditions brought about through the advance of civilization. . . . We were witnessing again that indescribably pathetic scene of love and longing for companionship . . . the heartbreaking picture of utter loneliness.

The single heath hen was never seen again after the early summer of 1931.

In June 1931 Grandpa and Dr. Gross took a nearly three-month trip to Labrador, along with Dr. Gross's son Bill and one of his students. They went to study the bird life of the north, especially the eider duck, a species making a splendid comeback from dangerously reduced numbers. They secured passage on a small coastal steamer making the first trip of the season from the city of Quebec to the Strait of Belle Isle. The cargo for small winter-starved ports of call included food, spare parts for engines, gasoline, and a Model T Ford. The captain of the crew was French Canadian, and the passengers represented many walks of life—lumbermen, fishermen, trappers, businessmen, salesmen, a small group of wealthy sportsmen from the States going up for the early salmon fishing, and a few women returning to homes or summer camps after a winter of city comforts. Grandpa described the trip:

In-vest-i-gate if you would know
That something is or isn't so.

> *The coast became more and more rugged, the villages far*
> *ther apart. At each stop some passengers disembarked.*
> *Now and then one bound farther along the coast came*
> *aboard. Day by day there was more chill in the air. Birds*
> *of the arctic fauna became more and more numerous—*
> *auks, murres, gannets, puffins, and eider ducks. Now*

and then a small mass of drifting ice was sighted. Our temporary base was located at Harrington Harbour, well up toward the Strait of Belle Isle, where is located the southernmost of the famous Grenfell hospitals on the Labrador coast, named for Labrador's great and justly famous missionary-physician, Sir Wilfred Grenfell. I was delighted and privileged to meet and spend many hours with this remarkable man.

All the filming and work we did with these northern birds was fascinating, but it was with the eider ducks that our greatest interest lay. We found the first nests in the "Green Forest," but not the Green Forest of my stories. Far, far from it. There trees forty to fifty years old, I was told, were little if any more than three feet high, if that. Beaten down by prevailing winds, flattened by the crushing weight of snow and ice for the larger part of the year, they formed a sort of thick green mat. Outside this, birches were for the same reason not trees in appearance but vines along the ground. So it was that almost literally I walked on, instead of in, the forest.

With a great deal of patience and discomfort Grandpa and Dr. Gross accomplished what they set out to do. Lying on their stomachs, motionless for hours at a time on the cold rocks, they managed to fully record on film the building of the eiders' nests, the hatching of the eggs, and the development of the ducklings.

Grandpa was truly in his element on this expedition, despite the strenuous effort required to record the ducks' behavior. He always yearned to return to Labrador and told me I could go with him if he ever returned. He knew I would appreciate it as much as he had. Though I later went to Labrador myself, I never had the chance to accompany him.

When I was ten years old, my best friend Anne's family invited me to spend a year in Oslo and Lillehammer, Norway, and to attend a boarding school there. They were leaving Hampstead for good. I wrote about the prospect in a letter to my grandparents:

Dear Nanna and Grandpa,

Sorry I haven't written sooner. Thanks a million times for all our Christmas presents. When are you coming back to visit us? If you come soon I will be home. But I think I am going to school in Norway for a year to be with my best friend Anne Kolsto, who is Norwegian. I am going across the North Sea on a boat all by myself. It is very rough, but it only takes one day and one night so it will be all right. Anne was run over by a car last week on our way home from school. We did not see the car coming because of the fog. Everyone pushed me out of the way, the ambulance came and took her away, and I was so scared, I ran all the way home and told Mummy who called Mrs. Kolsto right away. She was not hurt very badly and she is all right now.

Rosemary and I pass by the sweet shop on our way home from school every day, and yesterday we bought you some ginger because we had saved up money. Did you know that I got a new bike for Christmas? It's just what I wanted.

Robert is home on holiday, and he threw a stink bomb in the front hall. Everybody was mad. Daddy-Bill was the maddest and gave Robert a whacking. Robert was playing with his best friend Peter Dgkelly, and they play a lot of pranks together, but this one really smelled up the house.

Nanny got married. We were bridesmaids. She made us yellow fluffy dresses with ribbons and put flowers in our hair, and we walked down the aisle in front of her in a little church. Afterwards we had lemonade, little tiny tea sandwiches, and sweet cakes. We wish she hadn't gotten married though, because our new nurse is very strict. We have to march on the Heath. She wears a stiff white uniform and a white cap pinned on top of her hair which she cuts like a boy. Nobody likes her, not even Elsa our cook who likes everyone. Mummy told Elsa that Nurse is leaving day after tomorrow, and we are very glad because we are really scared of her.

Robert is going to Switzerland soon. We love Robert. It's fun when he comes home. He and Peter always

make us laugh. I hope Switzerland is a better place for
him as he spends too much time in the infirmary at
school. I hope he has fun there and gets to feel better.
I will try to write to you soon.
Know what? I love you.
Frances

Some of our friends thought I was too young to cross the North Sea by myself. They said to my mother, "Don't let her go across alone. It's too rough. It's a terrible sea to cross!" It is in fact more dangerous and rough than the Atlantic. But I wasn't afraid of the rough waters because Grandpa had written me a letter to encourage me, reminding me of his experience off the coast of Gloucester, Massachusetts. While working on an article on the fishing industry, he had been invited aboard a trawler to take some pictures of the men catching fish. He had never been on a boat on the open sea before and didn't know whether he would be seasick, but he wasn't afraid. He went out with the trawler one day when it was terribly rough, and he sat on the masthead and smoked his pipe while the boat rocked back and forth. The captain of the ship was impressed. "A man who can smoke a pipe on the masthead in a cross sea will never feed the fishes," he said.

Grandpa also reminded me that during his great journey to Labrador, the fog was thick, the seas were rough, the air was cold, and the ship was small. But he wouldn't have missed it for the world.

Grandpa always said, "Just say yes to opportunities in this world, providing they're not foolish or dangerous. If something appeals to you, just go do it. You'll find you can do things you never dreamed you could. You can do anything you want, if you want it enough," he used to say. "The chance of a new experience may never come again, so just do it."

So I thought, "If Mummy does let me, I want to go across the North Sea to Norway. I'll just go do it!" Grandpa thought it a fine idea, although he could not help but worry a bit and wrote, "Take very good care of yourself, my dear. Write me as soon as you arrive safely in Oslo."

The ship was ever so small, carrying only about seventy-five passengers, in comparison to the thousands that traveled on board a single ocean liner. It was very dark in my cabin, and most of the night I lay strapped in my bunk. But I could look out the porthole and watch the waves rushing by and the white foam splashing and the moon shedding its light on the water. The waves looked like dark pages of a book, turning over and over. Suddenly the porthole would fall below the waterline, and in the darkness I could see tiny creatures and seaweed sliding past in a pale green sea. I was entranced by this ever-changing watery spectacle. I wrote Grandpa as soon as I arrived and told him that I had not been sick at all because the crossing had been so exciting and the steward had taken good care of me.

I wrote to tell him how beautiful the mountains of Lillehammer were and how much he would like them. There was a brook with a lake at the bottom of it. We would swim in the lake in summer and skate on it in winter. In any season, we would hike cross-country through the mountains. I was a little homesick, but I loved my new friends and my new school.

Nobody ever shoveled snow in Norway, and I wrote this to Grandpa, who would shovel snow himself until he was eighty. "Dear Grandpa," I wrote, "it snows so much over here that you never have to shovel it because all we do is stomp it down with snowshoes and skis. If you lived over here you would never have to shovel snow again."

Grandpa and Nanna wrote to me often while I was in Norway, as they did whenever we children were away from them. Grandpa would send us poems and letters and stories. He liked to tell us how he missed us and fill us in on some of his and Nanna's adventures.

When I returned to England from Norway, I arrived after school had already begun. I hated my new boarding school, Channing House, outside London, which had been chosen for me at the last moment. I had a single room up on the third floor of the dormitory, probably because I was the last one enrolled. I was terribly lonely and felt abandoned. It was a traumatic time in my life. The other girls already had their friends, but my only friends were in Norway or back at Frognal, and I missed my brother and sisters. I didn't want to leave my room to go to class or to meals. I would look out the window at the pigeons and the sparrows flying about in the square below and talk to them. Grandpa wrote to me while I was there, but it did not seem to help much. I wanted to tell him how miserable I was, but I didn't dare because I thought he would be disappointed in me for complaining.

I was never petite or pretty, and I thought people found girls with such traits more acceptable. I did have one feature that brought me compliments—intense hazel blue eyes with long dark lashes. I was tall for my age and must have looked older than I was; it seemed more was expected of me than of other children my age. But I did know one thing—if I could make people laugh, things tended to get better. But at this boarding school I couldn't do that.

One evening Daddy-Bill, who had never paid much attention to me, called at the school to take me for a drive in a horse-drawn cab. It was cold and raining, and I could hardly believe that he had come to see me. He asked the cabby to stop for a moment, and he bought two bags of hot roasted chestnuts from a street vendor. We ate some during the ride back to the school, and even though I had never really liked them much, I pretended I did because I thought he was so wonderful to buy them for me. That visit seemed like a miracle to me. Up to that point, I had felt abandoned by my family. That night I put the remaining chestnuts under my pillow and wept. I slept that way every night until the remaining chestnuts had disintegrated into small bits and pieces.

In December of that year, 1933, my half-brother William

Standish Bradford, Jr., was born in Hampstead. My mother's dream of having a son with Bill, the man with whom she was completely obsessed from early courtship until his death in 1967, had been fulfilled. She, Bill, and William were now a family unto themselves—although since living in England my sisters and I have always been known as the Bradford girls.

Fortunately for me, however, several months later my stepfather was transferred back to the United States. When we came back to Massachusetts in 1934, my sisters and I were enrolled in the MacDuffie School for Girls in Springfield for the remainder of the school year. The furniture had not yet arrived for my parents' house at 47 Mulberry Street in Springfield, so while my stepfather, mother, little half-brother William, and his English nanny, whom we knew and loved as Nanny Brown, stayed together at the Bradford family home in Springfield, Robert, Rosemary, Jean, and I all stayed "at home" with our Nanna and Grandpa. I felt lonely no longer.

We had been in London during the years of the Great Depression. I didn't understand at the time how difficult that period had been for Grandpa and Nanna. In 1929, while we were in England, young Thornton and his wife Mildred had had a baby girl named Nancy. Thornton did not have a job at the time, and Mildred had to take a short leave of absence from her factory job. Grandpa helped them out financially, as they had little money, and when Mildred was able, she went back to work while Thornton took care of Nancy with the help of one of Mildred's sisters. Thornton adored Nancy and took her with him everywhere, as he was home most of the time without work. She in turn became very close to her father.

After the stock market crash in 1929, President Hoover earnestly proclaimed that the worst would be over in sixty days. Future president Franklin Roosevelt, then governor of New York, also believed the depression would be short-lived. However, as the years advanced into the 1930s, so did the hard times.

No home is ever mean or poor
Where love awaits you at the door.

Grandpa lost most of his savings in the crash and had difficulty earning enough to satisfy the demands on his bank account. A letter he wrote to his good friend Alfred Gross on October 31, 1929, suggests that, at least in this case, he was being betrayed by his innate optimism:

Dear Alfred:

Your letter on stocks just received. Sit tight. There is nothing else to do. Since you wrote your letter the worst has happened, I think. Yesterday's recovery was very satisfactory. You will note that your Telephone stock took a very nice rise. I am holding everything and shall con-tinue to hold them. I should not let Telephone stock go. It may take it a long time to get back to where it was, but it is, I believe, a stock to leave in your strong box indefinitely. I think there will be some good things come from this stock ultimately, as there have been in the past.

When the stock market broke a week ago last Monday, it looked to me as if a lot of stocks were down where they were bargains. I guess it looked the same way to a lot of other people. I went into the market on Tuesday and bought four stocks. I bought at the opening and they began to slump that day. On the final big slump on Tuesday of this week, I found that those stocks I had bought a week ago had shrunk by almost $26,000 in value. I had gone into the market with the expectation of making a quick turn of a thousand or two. Now I am wondering how long it is going to take me to get out at what I went in at. Let me say, however, that I am not worrying. . . .

This market has wonderfully demonstrated the need of owning one's stocks. If the stocks are inherently good, the owners need not lose any sleep no matter how low the price drops. You understand, of course, that these low prices do not reflect in any way the value of good stocks. These good stocks have been thrown overboard by people who had big margined accounts and who had to sacrifice their good stocks in order to meet their margins. The more of these stocks thrown on the market, the greater the break in prices, naturally.

To show you just what happened, let me say that on

my list I had nineteen stocks. All but two or three of these had been showing me handsome profits. On Tuesday of this week I had just two of the nineteen that were showing me any profits and the profits on these were, of course, terribly reduced. All the rest show a loss. But I am not losing any sleep. Already Telephone has come back to above what I paid for it. I haven't checked up the others to see if any more have crept over the line.

I am delighted to know that the ruffed grouse continue to come in. That is bully. We will say a word more next Saturday evening. My hour has been changed from 7:30 Wednesdays to seven o'clock Saturday evening. A week ago Wednesday, while you were away, I announced this change and asked if the unseen audience would fol-low me to Saturday, and hinted that I had considered it might possibly be well to discontinue the talks. I wish you could have seen the mail that poured in this past week. I received 1,025 letters representing 3,000 to 4,000 people. They contained some marvelous tributes that quite overwhelmed me.

Lady joins me in sending our best to you and Edna. Sincerely yours,
Thornton

Nanna, either by shrewd intuition or good advice, had liq-uidated her personal stock holdings in September 1929 and had bought gold, thereby suffering no losses. Later she rein-vested in stocks and bonds as the New York Stock Exchange and the world economy regained stability. It never occurred to Grandpa to wonder how Nanna kept up with her obligations at home and to all of us living in London. She had always been frugal and alert to a good bargain. Grandpa trusted her ability to keep their household running smoothly.

Nanna kept the winter woolens in an old trunk from which the smell of mothballs escaped as she lifted the lid in autumn, and I remember Grandpa smelling of camphor at the beginning of the cold weather every year. Nanna had determination in abundance; clothes were mended so neatly that the darnings were almost works of art. Old worn trousers were patched until they consisted of little else but patches on patches. She drove miles to save a penny on groceries.

Grandpa felt he had to pay everyone else's debts in the family. "I seem to be working constantly only to bail other people out of their financial problems," he wrote in his diary. "I am worried over Chester, fearful that he might go off or do something desperate because of his business troubles. I went to his office to buck him up. I told him that Nanna and I would see him through. Why is the present generation so unable to stand alone? Have worked hard all my life chiefly to support others and still must keep it up."

The dependency of his children and in-laws sometimes angered Grandpa, yet he couldn't help but assist them. About his biological son, Thornton, he felt most torn. "What man can bear to fall into such darkness?" he wrote. "I despair of myself. I do not act with humility and reverence for other men. I am full of anger and disappointment. How could I have such a son?" Elsewhere the diary moans, "A letter from son—knocked all the life out of me. No job, Mildred sick, no money for food. Even though he hates me, he must come to me for help." Grandpa's work ethic was so strong, he didn't see why anybody should ever be without some kind of job. After all, one can sweep the streets or even do errands for others. One doesn't have to start from the top. He never could understand why his son didn't work and was constantly in trouble.

In 1931, Grandpa was shocked to learn that his own granddaughter Nancy, now two years old, had developed poliomyelitis and had been paralyzed for about a week, with the result that she was unable to walk because of badly deformed feet. Ultimately, she needed eleven operations to correct her condition. Late that December, Grandpa received a wire from Thornton saying that Mildred was in the hospital in serious condition. Their new baby had been born dead that morning, and Mildred was very ill. During this time Mildred's sister Eva took care of Nancy. Thornton and Mildred seemed plagued by trouble.

For their part, Thornton and Mildred must have wondered why my own family was living so well. We had so much more than they did. I'm not sure they knew why or how close we were to Grandpa, for there was little communication between them and us grandchildren. Our immediate family had all the money we needed, and they had very little, although Mildred had close relatives who, thankfully, afforded them some stability. And whenever they needed anything desperately, Grandpa helped them.

Chapter Four

*A*S WE APPROACHED
Laughing Brook again in
1934 after having been away so long, we watched for the
giant elms, which stood tall enough to be seen from a great
distance. We knew that beneath them stood the gray shingled
house with tiny-paned windows shining in the sun and window boxes filled with pink geraniums. The familiar barn, the
tiny guest house with its little porch overhanging the brook,
and Grandpa's house on the hill would be waiting for us.

As we always did when we arrived at Laughing Brook, we
raced across the grass past the well sweep and through the door
into the old eighteenth-century kitchen. It was the largest
room in the house, with what in the eyes of the young was a
huge red-brick fireplace and surrounding hearth on the south
wall, formerly used for cooking as well as heating. On the left
stood Grandpa's chair and the side table where he kept his
reading lamp, his book, and his pipe. A card table stood across
the room, always ready for a game of hearts, and an ancient
wireless stood on the table by the east window. There we would
listen to Grandpa's broadcasts, as well as "The Shadow,"

"Fibber McGee and Molly," and young people's symphonic music conducted by Walter Damrosch. Grandpa was never present during these interludes, but he rarely missed the evening news with commentator Lowell Thomas. (I can still hear his sign-off: "So long until tomorrow!") In the *New York Herald Tribune* editorials written by Walter Lippmann, a man he greatly admired, Grandpa followed the news of the day.

A home is always what you make it. With love there you will ne'er forsake it.

The modern kitchen, which once had been the woodshed, was to the right of the main door. On the left was a large dining room with a Franklin stove and a round applewood table, surrounded by eight small antique chairs and a tall ladder-backed chair in the corner. The dining room also had a capacious sideboard and a corner cupboard. The wallpaper was blue and white to match the china, some of which was displayed about the room.

Beyond the large north window of the old kitchen, opposite the fireplace, was the door to the pantry, where Nanna kept her best china and glassware. Another door, two steps down from the pantry, led into the root cellar, which had been dug out of the hillside. It was neatly lined with bricks and had a hard dirt floor and covered chimney. Here Nanna kept garden vegetables and jars of homemade jellies, jams, pickles, and vegetables that she put up each summer.

100

Opposite the main entrance to the old kitchen was a small room. To its left a door led into the parlor. The furnishings of this room included a Franklin stove with a Dresden shepherd and shepherdess placed on the mantel above it, a love seat, a high-backed wing chair covered with softly colored flowered chintz, several rocking chairs, a ladder-back armchair, tilt-top tables, two little sewing tables, and a collection of small Florentine paintings hanging on the gray landscape wallpaper. In the corner by the bay window stood a slant-topped *escritoire,* or secretary. From every window in the house hung white ruffled curtains.

A boxed-in stairway led to the upstairs rooms. The steps were five inches deep and narrow in width. The first four turned the corner, the next six went straight up, and the last four steps branched left and right, leading to two bedroom doors, each with a leather thong for lifting its latch. When we were small we could climb these steep, steep stairs facing straight ahead, but as we grew older, we had to step up with our feet turned sideways.

Under the high, pitched roof, the east bedroom had twin beds, a curtained lavatory, and windows looking across to the barn, the brook, and the guest house. The west bedroom was Grandpa's and Nanna's. They had a double sleigh-backed bed with posts carved in a pineapple pattern, a bureau desk with a folding writing shelf (cabinets above and drawers below) situated between two windows overlooking the meadow, and a large pink and white bathroom.

In the old kitchen at Laughing Brook, we sat around the fireplace and told stories. We lit the fire and waited for a spark to land in front of one of us. That person had to tell a story, and the story had to be true. Grandpa wrote a book about this family tradition, called *While the Story Log Burns.* He was careful to say that the stories we told were true.

One day he reached over and poked the fire. A big spark shot out and landed near Rosemary's feet. "I don't know a story," my sister said, "except maybe about Grandpa's cat."

She continued, "It was a cat Grandpa had when he was a little boy, and he said that every word of this story is true. The cat's name was Clover, and it was given to Grandpa when it was a kitten. Grandpa was very fond of it and taught it a number of tricks. It would jump through a loop made with his arms, and it would play dead when told to. All but the tip of the tail would stay still, but the tip would always move.

Much may be gained by sitting still If you but have the strength of will.

"Clover used to sleep with Grandpa, and his mother didn't approve of it. So one afternoon she said, 'I'm not going to have Clover sleeping with you any more. From now on, he's got to find some place to sleep other than your bed.' Clover was sitting nearby at the time. Late in the afternoon he disappeared, and at supper time he couldn't be found, although he was always on hand then.

"Grandpa had to go to bed at eight o'clock. Before going, he went to the door and called and called, but no Clover appeared. After the light went out and he was almost ready to go to sleep, he heard a thump underneath the bed, and a few seconds later Clover was up on the bed and snuggling up to Grandpa's neck. He had been hiding among the bedsprings on one of the slats."

My little sister Jean piped up, "Do you suppose Clover knew what your mother said, Grandpa?"

He answered with his usual chuckle. "Perhaps it was just coincidence that Clover picked that day to form the habit of hiding among the springs of the bed. We never know just how much animals understand and sense what we say. But it is a true story."

Then a spark jumped out and landed near him, and he went on:

"This story is true in every particular, and I will tell it to you exactly as it was told to me by an officer in the division of United States regulars. It is difficult to associate so beautiful and dainty a creature as a deer with the horrors of warfare, yet this one was right on the battlefront during the First World War. Here is the story.

"Fitz is what the boys named him, and he was born near Hill 204, northwest of Château-Thierry about June 6, 1918. He was a dwarf French deer, and probably was only hours old when a member of Company B, Seventh Machine Battalion, Third United States Division, picked him up after his mother had been scared away by shell fire. The cook raised him on canned condensed milk and other rations that only an army cook could obtain.

"This small deer was thought much of by all the men, and went with them through all the battles from the Marne to the Rhine. From one of the French gas masks, a special mask was made for Fritz. He was French by birth, but was thoroughly American by adoption, and he was a soldier through and through. He would have nothing whatsoever to do with the civilians, or with allied soldiers. He would only come to a man in an American uniform. On the Rhine he disappeared. It was suspected and hoped that, having fraternized with some German deer, he found a sweetheart and eloped.

"That is the story, one of the few pleasant stories of the Great War. No one knows to how great an extent he helped by his trusting confidence to preserve the morale of his fighting comrades. Who loves animals must also love his fellow man, and when such love becomes universal, there will be no more wars."

One day I picked up a blue feather that had been dropped by Sammy Jay. I thought it so pretty that I showed it to Grandpa. When it was my turn to tell a story around the fire, I talked about my find. My brother and sisters asked what was so great about a feather: "There are lots of feathers around just like it. Birds are always losing their feathers."

"I know," I said, "but this is different, I . . . he floated it down from his favorite branch like a present, and it landed right next to me."

Grandpa came to my rescue: "Some things seem ordinary and commonplace because they are so familiar to us that we look at them, but don't see them. Most things about us are truly marvelous. Look under the microscope at this feather that Frances has brought us."

We did so, as he talked on: "You see, it looks as if made up of two rows of featherlets on opposite sides of the quill. Look sharp and you will see that each of these featherlets, which are called barbs, has two rows of what are called barbules, and these barbules have tiny curved hooks called barbicels. This feather is about six inches long, and that means it has about twelve hundred barbs or featherlets, and as each of these has about two hundred and seventy-five pairs of barbules, there are almost a million barbules on this one feather, not to mention the tiny barbicels."

Two eyes you have
bright as can be.
Perhaps some day
you'll learn to see.

All this took a good deal of time as we took turns looking through the microscope, trying desperately to see and understand what Grandpa was showing us. It was a lot to swallow in one gulp. The old kitchen was silent, except for the crackling of the fire, as we all thought of the mystery and intricacies of this small blue feather.

Then I picked up my blue feather and looked at it with a

mixture of pride and awe. "It's marvelous. It's . . . it's beautiful!" I exclaimed. "Isn't it!"

On still, warm summer days when the windows were open wide in the house on the hill where Grandpa worked, Laughing Brook murmured a soft accompaniment to the clicking of his typewriter. We were always welcome in his house on the hill, where on his desk he kept jars of different-colored hard candy, especially his favorite, sugared ginger. Although tempted to barge in often, we knew that he was working, and Nanna wouldn't let us run up there constantly. Every time we did, though, he would smile and say, "Oh, come in, come in, my dears. Help yourselves to a piece of candy." I never once felt that we were an intrusion.

The door to this building opened into one large room, where windows on every side overlooked the brook, the green meadows, the forest, and the purple hills of the Berkshires in the distance. The windowsills held many small feathered, ceramic, carved, and cast-iron birds and animals. Hanging from the studs on the brown, knotted, unlined walls were several paintings by Harrison Cady. Stacks of books (including a large, dog-eared Bible) were placed on various tables, one of which was large and round and

How fortunate that in life's game So few have talents just the same.

covered with a fringed, multicolored hand-woven shawl. Two filing cabinets, a bookcase, and boxes filled with papers stood against a wall, and small oriental rugs were scattered about the floor. Near the wall opposite the door was a black pot-bellied stove, a coal bucket containing kindling, a poker, a shovel, and a small stack of wood. Next to it a door led onto a porch. Logs were stacked against the outer wall, and a wicker rocking chair invited one to sit there and admire the view.

When we youngsters had climbed the hill and reached the house, we would carefully peek through the open door to see our grandfather sitting at his mahogany desk. Using only his two index fingers, he would be tapping out a story or letter on his ancient Remington manual typewriter.

In unabashed delight we would run in, knocking each other about to be the first to give him a hug. We inspected the whole room, examining this and that, and even looking high in the rafters to see how many spiders were spinning their silken webs. We asked questions about Peter Rabbit, Jimmy Skunk, Grandfather Frog, Paddy the Beaver, Jerry Muskrat, Johnny Chuck, Reddy Fox, Danny Meadow Mouse, Billy Mink, Little Joe Otter, Sammy Jay, and Blacky the Crow, and Grandpa happily laughed at our enthusiasm, saying, "Come over here where you can sit close, and I will tell you about Billy Mink's swimming party, because I know on this warm day you will be down in the brook as soon as Nanna will let you."

There was quite a population of native trout in Laughing

Brook, not very large, only six to eight inches long, but Grandpa liked to fish, and before anyone else was up he would catch his breakfast by the bridge where a couple of good spots had been dammed up. Then he cooked them up for his breakfast.

My sister Rosemary caught him one morning sitting at the breakfast table with watery, bloodshot eyes and a running nose, which he wiped with a large white handkerchief. All the while he was eating trout with some vegetables from the garden. Rosemary picked up the bottle on the table and discovered that it was Tabasco sauce. "Golly, Grandpa," she asked, "how much of this did you put on your fish?" He would not admit he had overdone it and kept right on eating and weeping as though nothing was wrong, chuckling through his tears as if his food was just the way he wanted it. Grandpa could be very stubborn.

Nobody could cook scrambled eggs like Grandpa, and every time we came to visit, we asked him to make them for us for breakfast. He cooked them in the double boiler while we waited and watched, and they were always soft, custardy, and delicious. Another of his specialties was quahog chowder. Nobody could make this like Grandpa or Nanna. There was always a pot ready on the stove when they knew we were arriving.

Mr. Green, the caretaker who lived close by, helped Grandpa with the large vegetable garden. We would all pick corn there. Grandpa would roast the corn over an open fireplace outside; then he would cook hamburg, onions, and peppers in a big frying pan over an open fire. I loved watching him prepare food over the fire. He usually did this near twilight when it was quite still, except for the crackling of the fire and the children chattering away.

Nanna used to blow on a large pink-and-white conch shell to command attention to the main house—announcing mealtimes, the mail, guest arrivals, a phone call, or anything of importance. The sound could be heard high on the hill, to the far end of the big meadow, past the apple orchard, and all along Laughing Brook. No one but our grandmother could produce from this beautiful shell such a resonant trumpet-like sound. We all tried to imitate it, but to no avail. She told us it was the sound the Titans of Greek mythology had made when they blew on their conch shells, simulating the glorious sounds of a thousand trumpets.

On Earth below, in Heaven above, The one most precious thing is love.

One summer, three little chucks were found orphaned and were brought to Grandpa by some neighborhood children. Grandpa kept them just long enough for us to enjoy and play with them and for them to learn to forage for themselves. That did not take much more than a week, as they learned quickly and got fat and bold. He then set them free, feeling sure they could have a better life on their own.

Contents of the packages people sent Grandpa in the mail often contained surprises. We were always eager to find out what was in them. Nanna would blow the conch shell when one arrived, and Grandpa would hear it in his studio up on the hill. He would drop everything he was doing to get the mail. He loved corresponding with so many people. Sometimes the quantity of mail was staggering.

My grandparents always lived modestly. They both loved the outdoors, fishing, camping, and gardening. Nanna also belonged to a bridge club. At home Nanna cooked pies and casseroles for church suppers while Grandpa was working up on the hill. Grandpa always went along to the church suppers, but rarely attended church otherwise. In truth he would rather be outdoors working in the garden or on the hill or wandering in the woods, where in silence his own spiritual longings were fulfilled.

In his humility, Grandpa felt Nanna should have married a more sophisticated man of literature and travel, instead of sharing his secluded, simple life. They were often invited by the Cadys to travel with them to Europe, China, and other exotic and exciting places, but as much as Grandpa wanted to accompany them and take his "Lady," he felt time would not permit it. He felt compelled by his destiny to keep working in his chosen field.

Chapter Five

*I*N THE SPRING OF 1933, while we were still in England, Grandpa wrote to us announcing that Thornton W. Burgess IV had been born and was as healthy as could be, although Mildred had needed an operation to pull her through. Grandpa was praying for her and knew that God would take care of her. His prayers were answered, and two years later she had a third child, David.

Shortly after David's birth, Thornton III abandoned Mildred and their three children without leaving a forwarding address. Mildred told their daughter, little Nancy, that her father had died of tuberculosis. There had been a history of the disease in the Burgess family. Nancy could not understand why her father was no longer there, and this answer was all that Mildred could think of at the time.

Thornton wrote to Grandpa occasionally to ask for financial help, and after much continued difficulty in California, he enlisted in the army. In 1943 he wrote Grandpa that he would be "on the high seas" by Christmas. He asked his father to send him Mildred's address so that he could write to his daughter, Nancy. He was stationed in the Philippines and after his discharge from the service went to work in Saudi Arabia as an executive technician for the Arabian-American Oil Company. Eventually, he returned to the United States.

Among Grandpa's personal papers was a poem he wrote for Thornton:

WHAT MATTERS

Perhaps your necktie is askew—
  What matter?
Perhaps your pants are wrinkled too—
  What matter?
Perhaps your shoes a polish need,
Or maybe they have not been treed—
  What matter?

Perhaps your coat is not quite new—
  What matter?
Or just a trifle small for you—
  What matter?
Perhaps there is a hint of shine
Upon your trousers' seat, like mine—
  What matter?

But what you are and what you do
  Does matter.

The inner self that's really you
    Does matter.
That you should do the best you can
And thus to prove you are a man
    Does matter.

"As much as I love you," he would say to us step-grand-children, putting his arms about us, "where are my own?" I wasn't aware of the degree of his sadness until after I was back at school in the United States. Then I realized that he wasn't just a wonderful person who never had heavy burdens to carry. Each with our own troubles, we grew even closer.

Once when we were at Laughing Brook, a little boy brought a baby skunk that was near death and gave it to Grandpa in hopes that the animal might be saved. Grandpa kept Jimmy Skunk for over a year. He had never been de-scented, yet remained tame and never once perfumed the air. Jimmy trusted Grandpa and followed him in the garden, the meadow, the forest, the hill, and the house. Sometimes he took a ride with him in the Packard. He would even crawl up his pant leg and sleep on top of his knee until it was time for bed. Grandpa felt a great deal of affection for that little skunk. He said, "Animals, I am convinced, love to make us human ani-

A danger past is a
    danger past,
So why not just for-
    get it?
Watch out instead
    for the one ahead
Until you've safely
    met it.

113

mals laugh, and they are often well aware, I am convinced, of what makes us do so."

Grandpa once said, "The skunk is native only to America. It lives nowhere else in the world. America should drop the eagle as a national emblem and substitute the skunk. This idea shocks some people, but did you ever study Jimmy Skunk? Jimmy is armed for defense, not offense. He is absolutely independent. He asks no favors. He minds his own business. He is absolutely unafraid. He knows his rights and stands up for them. Even a bear will step aside for Jimmy Skunk."

During one of our summer visits, the roots of one of the largest elm trees outside the kitchen at Laughing Brook began to lift the floor, while the tree itself darkened the kitchen considerably. Grandpa finally had it cut down. Soon after the tree was removed, Jimmy the Skunk became very ill. Grandpa wondered what in the world was the matter with him. The next day his condition grew worse, so Grandpa took him to the vet, who thought he had been poisoned. After Jimmy died it was discovered that the men who had cut the tree down had put poison on the tree stump to make it dissolve. Jimmy had apparently eaten grubs from the poisoned trunk. Grandpa blamed himself and mourned over Jimmy's death. "Why didn't I know they put poison there?" he asked himself. "Why wasn't I more alert?"

Within weeks of Jimmy's death Grandpa learned that his son Thornton had been put in jail in California. Grandpa had financed Thornton's purchase of a gasoline station, which Thornton had mishandled, leaving him unable to pay his debts. In those days, bankruptcy was punishable by a jail sentence.

Grandpa sobbed unabashedly when he heard the news. "God damn it," he said, "how could I have had such a son?!" He blew his nose on the large white handkerchief that always protruded from his back trouser pocket. "I will write him a letter telling him what I think. I shall try not to preach, as it does no good, but I hope this sentence to jail will teach him a new way of thinking."

That night I lay on my bed, feeling acutely sad. How unjust everything was! I felt terribly alone and cried for the whole world. I cried for Grandpa, for Nanna, for my brothers and my sisters. I cried for the beauty of the stars in the night sky. I cried for little Jimmy Skunk and for all the animals and people on the earth. I wondered if God cried as I did.

Grandpa blamed himself for Thornton's unhappiness. He chastised himself for not having been home when Thornton was young, for being driven to his writing, for missing his son's childhood. He didn't recognize the immensely positive effect his love had on my siblings and me, and what troubled and dissatisfied people we might have become without him. He had also contributed to the joy and happiness of so many others.

Grandpa's behavior toward other people and animals clearly spoke a moral message as loud and clear as those in any of his writings. But in his own self-assessment, he judged himself inadequate. He knew it was easier to write about morality than to live by it. He knew that at times he hadn't listened well or had failed in empathic understanding or had missed an opportunity to take a strong moral stance. He recognized these failures with regret but continued to be kind and loving and never stopped trying to be a better person. But he forever mourned the loss of his son.

During our early years of moving back and forth across the Atlantic, being transferred in and out of schools, my sister Rosemary expressed our plight by saying, in both anger and amusement, that we children were "flotsam and jetsam." The years immediately following our return from London in 1934 were especially hard for me. I was plagued with eczema around my eyes, ears, mouth, and neck, and my arms were bandaged. The skin was thick, cracked, and bleeding. Each morning, in order to open my eyes, I had to bath my eyelids to wash away the crust formed overnight. I itched and scratched in discomfort and was ashamed of my awful appearance. Despite everything, Grandpa always made me feel beautiful and optimistic. He would tell me with a hug, "It will soon be all right again; and besides, it's what's inside your dear self that counts."

When doubtful what course to pursue 'Tis sometimes best to nothing do.

I became more unsettled and nervous, changed boarding schools several times in the years following, and did some things as a teenager that disappointed Grandpa. He let me know that I was inconsiderate, unreliable. A typical remonstrance from him was "You are too apt to let absorption in your own selfish concerns govern you. You did not acknowledge the receipt of this month's allowance. This is not a reproach, but a reminder. You forget those who love you dearly."

I felt so terrible for disappointing him that I was extremely repentant and told him how sorry and ungrateful I felt. Once, while home from boarding school on an Easter holiday, I didn't want to return to school, so I purposely missed the train. Grandpa was very angry with me. He didn't understand why I would do such a thing. I didn't know why I had done it either. Maybe I was being defiant, hoping that if I shut my eyes the impending separation and loneliness would just go away and I could stay home. The next day, however, I was duly packed off.

Now and then some humble pie Is good for everyone to try.

I'm not sure that Grandpa understood that I suffered from confusion and insecurity. We four children had much money spent on us, especially for excellent private educational opportunities and other privileges that he had never enjoyed, but we were hurt by being shuffled around from place to place. Nevertheless he was certain that we should be nothing but grateful. I recall Grandpa saying to me, "My dear, we do not live in the world we would like to, but rather in the world that has been imposed upon us. We do not do everything we desire, but only that which we can and are allowed to do."

During those troubled years I would even shut out my grandfather, unable to bear the burden of trying to win his approval, or anyone's approval. I felt vaguely guilty for something that I couldn't put my finger on. I was often lonely and apathetic. I seemed to spend my life searching for a place to belong, and the only security I had known was with my grandparents.

I had always had a penchant for horses and the smell of stables. At the riding school next to my school in New York, I had fallen in love with a beautiful chestnut mare that happened to be for sale. I wrote to Nanna asking her to buy her for me. I promised to keep her in the barn at Laughing Brook and take care of her by myself. Grandpa couldn't understand this at all. "That will not be practical, my dear," he said.

But I wouldn't give up. I begged, I pleaded, I made promises. I would be no trouble at all; I would take care of the horse; I would muck out the stall; I would do everything they asked if only they would let me come back and keep my horse on their farm. Grandpa wrote in his diary, "That girl just won't take no for an answer. I don't know what's gotten into her." I never told him that my request was as much an excuse to come home and be near them as it was a wish to own that beautiful chestnut mare.

I finally admitted that all I wanted was to attend school

near them. Realizing this, my mother let me board at the MacDuffie School for Girls in Springfield, where I had been a day student when I first came back from England. At last I was happy and felt at home in that school near my beloved Grandpa and Nanna. I spent weekends with them. They would drive in to pick me up until I was sixteen, when Nanna gave me a little Ford convertible so I could drive myself back and forth.

The MacDuffie School was small and had a homelike atmosphere. Everyone knew everyone else, teachers and students alike. There were only twelve girls in my class, and I was chosen class president. I also was voted student government president and captain of the "red team." (The school had two teams, red and blue, that played against each other in hockey, baseball, basketball, and lacrosse.) I also enjoyed acting, though I often had trouble remembering my lines.

One special event stands out in my adolescent years. Grandpa and Nanna's good friends Dr. and Mrs. Gross and their family arranged for us to spend a weekend at their home in Brunswick, Maine (where Dr. Gross taught at Bowdoin College). Their youngest son, Tom, a sophomore, would escort me to the Saturday night dance at Bowdoin, featuring Artie Shaw's band. Tom was a good sport about taking me along, as I was only fifteen, though I looked older and loved to dance. Tom had persuaded his friends to show me a good time, so I was hardly able to dance with one boy for a few minutes before another cut in. At one point I got up on stage with one of the boys and sang a duet of the popular song "Who," and blushed with pride when Artie Shaw congratulated us on our perfect singing. The dance ended at eleven-thirty and we returned home. It was a glorious evening.

These years with Grandpa and Nanna, while I attended the MacDuffie School, were the best of my young life. In the spring, Grandpa and I would don our rubber boots and wander beside the freshwater marsh near Laughing Brook. There stood the disheveled remnants of autumn's cattails which looked like fat brown velvet-covered sticks in summer. During the winter many of these flower heads (each holds as many as 125,000 tufted seeds) had burst, releasing seeds to fly in the air like clouds of gossamer down. Mice harvest some of the fluff, using it to insulate their winter shelters. Birds and other animals line their nests with it. In the summer the muskrat feeds on the plant's stems and leaves; in the autumn it uses the stalks for building its home. In the winter the muskrat is always warm below the ice, eating cattail roots and rhizomes. In the springtime, the shoots of new green cattail leaves must be as welcome a treat to the muskrat as the first vegetables of spring are to us.

We could hear from the top of the big hickory tree a call that went "Quong-ka-ree! Quong-ka-ree! Quong-ka-ree! " I knew it was Redwing the Blackbird, for there is no other song quite like his, and he is one of the first to arrive in the spring. We watched him fly down from his high perch and alight among the broken-down bulrushes to nest. As he flew, we could see the beautiful red patch on the bend of each wing. When he landed, Mrs. Redwing flew to another spot close by. She wore no bright-colored shoulder patches. In fact, she hadn't a bright feather anywhere and dressed in grayish brown streaked with darker brown, almost black.

We could hear spring peepers, wood frogs, and other awakening creatures announcing their presence, and we could see insects flying about for the redwing to feed on. We occasionally saw marsh wrens, rails, and ring-necked ducks, and we listened to and watched the flit and chip of a swamp sparrow. Grandpa and I would gaze over the marsh for a long while. Sometimes the great blue heron would come to find fish.

When it was time to wander home along the brook, Grandpa and I would talk quietly and happily about what we had seen, and he would remind me of the importance of the water and the marshes. He would say, "You know, Frances, in biblical imagery water represents life and salvation. In scientific and ecological fact, as well, water is the basis of life. The marshes are often referred to as the cradle of life, where all life begins. Without water, there would be no life. We must be careful with it."

All year round, we walked along the paths in the woods, looking for the birds and animals that occupied the dead trees. In the spring we could sometimes find the nest of a bluebird, a red-breasted nuthatch, a downy woodpecker, a starling, a flying squirrel, a porcupine, carpenter ants, and honey bees. We would watch the nuthatch ferry food into a tiny hole high in a white pine tree during all four seasons of the year; they and the "downies" scoured the bark for insects, larvae, and eggs.

I liked to help Grandpa with his typing. At Laughing Brook on early, still summer mornings, I walked barefoot through the kitchen door onto the cool, dewy grass with the sheen of early morning mist covering the landscape. As I approached the steep stepping stones to Grandpa's house on the hill, I sometimes heard only the drilling of a woodpecker breaking the silence. I knew Grandpa would be there waiting for me, for he was always up before anyone else.

When I was home with Grandpa while attending MacDuffie's, we talked a great deal about religion. Grandpa was deeply ecumenical, believing that the infinite is the source of all being, no matter what name different religions put to this infinite source. He believed that one should honor and learn from vastly different beliefs, and that one should not try to convert the other or try to bring all religions into a common system. "I seriously wonder," he said, "whether compassion is not the one value that every major religious faith of the world wants to teach its believers, in spite of

Who for more knowledge never tries Will never be accounted wise.

everything that causes hostility." Grandpa would have appreciated the words so beautifully voiced in 1988 by Joanna Macy: "From Judaism, Christianity, and Islam to Hinduism, Buddhism, Taoism, and Native American and Goddess religions, each offers images of the sacred web into which we are woven. We are called children of one God and 'members of one body.' We are seen as drops in the ocean of Brahman. We are pictured as jewels in the Net of India. We interexist—like synapses in the mind of an all-encompassing being."

Grandpa believed and taught me to believe, as the Native Americans do, in the interconnectedness of all things. Chief Seattle (1786?–1866), of the Suquamish Indians, wrote, "Whatever befalls the earth befalls the sons of the earth. What is man without the beasts? If all the beasts were gone, man would die from a great loneliness of spirit. For whatever happens to the beasts, soon happens to man. All things are connected."

Grandpa and I talked about how every molecule, every part of us, is exactly the same as what's in a leaf or a blade of grass; we can't separate ourselves from the rest of nature. He often referred to chloroplasts and mitochondria, two organelles that are in a fundamental sense the most important living things on earth, as they produce oxygen for all living things. They are the same, whether they are in me, in seagulls, in dune grass, in whales, in trees or dogs or skunks. Through them we are connected.

Another Native American, Black Elk, wrote, "We should

understand well that all things are the works of the Great Spirit. . . . We should know that He is within all things, the trees, the grasses, the rivers, the mountains, and all the four-legged animals, and the winged peoples; and even more important, we should understand that He is also above all these things and peoples."

We enjoyed the abundance of Old and New Testament metaphor—from the Psalms, the Proverbs, and the parables of Jesus. Later, as he grew older, Grandpa and I talked about death. He said, and I sincerely agreed, that after death we would become part of the cosmic dust—stardust, we used to call it—with all souls intertwined in a rebirth of joy. I have always considered that a lovely description. He often repeated excerpts from the Psalms whose message was "help me" or "forgive me" or "I wish I could have done better." But most of the Psalms he read and referred to in his life offered praise and thanksgiving for all creation.

After Grandpa received an honorary doctorate of letters (Litt.D.) from Northeastern University in Boston in 1938, I began addressing all his letters to Dr. Thornton W. Burgess, and I introduced him to others as Dr. Burgess.

At the end of my senior year at MacDuffie's, my classmates and I were preparing for examinations and making plans for the future. Leaving the school was terrifying. Once again, sadness and apprehension overcame me concerning what life might hold for me. For a while I had been a big frog in a small pond, and I did not want to move on. It was what Grandpa described as a period of darkness. What was I going to do?

For graduation, Grandpa presented me with John Burroughs's book *A Year in the Field,* accompanied by the following dedication:

TO FRANCES
To one who finds the sunlight's gold,
The silver in the rain;
For whom the humblest flower blows;
Who hears the glad refrain
Of all the woodland choristers
And asks no greater boon
Than just to stray through forest aisles
With heart in glad atune;
To one to whom the mountains speak;
For whom the rivers sing;
Who sees in autumn's falling leaves
The promise of the spring;
To whom the secret of the trees
Is told above the brook;
To such a one, a comrade, I
Make offer of this book.
Grandpa, June 1940

Eventually, it was decided that I should try the Katherine Gibbs School in Boston for the school year 1940–41, to

improve my secretarial skills. I secretly hoped that I could
become Grandpa's secretary. I had typed for him and had
thought it so much fun helping him write stories and the
short moral aphorisms that introduced them, some of which I
have sprinkled in the margins of this book.
When I occasionally came up with an idea,
he would say, "Oh, Frances, that's bully!
That's the one we're going to use!
That's much better than I could
do." I felt overjoyed when he
praised me. But it was, of course,
unrealistic to think I could be his
secretary. I may have mentioned it
in passing, but we never discussed
it seriously.

*Thus always you
will meet the test
To do the thing you
do the best.*

    My stepfather had told me, as
Grandpa's grandfather, Charles Burgess, had told
him, "Don't bother to go to college. Go somewhere where you
can learn to earn a living and be independent." He and my
mother had moved to Taunton, Massachusetts, south of
Boston, where I went to live after I left Katherine Gibbs in
1941 and secured a temporary job in a bank at Camp Miles
Standish, an army base nearby. My parents were seldom
home, and my brothers and sisters were gone, leaving only the
cook and Allen the chauffeur at the far end of the house. I
visited my grandparents as often as I could, in spite of
wartime gas rationing during World War II.

Camp Miles Standish was a staging area for troops from different locations, awaiting orders for deployment to their next military assignments. Some of the men and women stayed for a week, and some for a few months. One of my duties as a member of the Social Service Committee was to greet the incoming personnel, most of them young and far from home. One day a group of Royal Air Force flyers arrived. That evening the Social Service women greeted them at a small dinner. Opposite me sat a young Australian lieutenant, Gordon Balcombe. Our eyes kept turning toward each other during dinner, at first rather shyly, but then in a natural and comfortable exchange of glances. Soon we were talking, oblivious to those around us. He asked if he could see me the following day.

The gentle expression of joy on his face when we met the next day made me feel as though a waterfall of pure, cool, sparkling water was softly washing over me. I not only saw him that day, but every day for a magical two and a half months. My feelings of loneliness disappeared. I felt happy and free as he held my hand while we walked for miles in the woods and in the town. We laughed and sang and hugged and kissed like innocent children.

Twice, we saved enough gas coupons to drive to Hampden to visit Nanna and Grandpa. My grandmother remarked, when she later called me on the telephone, "What a lovely young man, so tall and handsome, and he has such a lovely way with him." Grandpa said, "A nice young man. Could fit

127

in anywhere. Too bad he must go off to war. None of these valiant young men and women should have to go to war. I shall pray very hard, my dear, for his return when it is all over, for I like him very much."

Gordon and I were inseparable and terribly in love. We did not speak of the day that would soon come for him to leave. We spoke only of the now and the bright future that might lie ahead. When his day of departure finally came, we clung to each other for a few moments, and then he was gone.

Two weeks went by. I received a telegram from him, saying, "I love you!—Gordon." Another two weeks passed and a telegram was sent to me by his best friend. "Gordon's plane shot down over Germany. Gordon killed. . . ." Even though news of the war left little doubt that most of our flyers would never come home, I did not want to believe that Gordon would be one of them. I was unable to think of the future without him, even though my time with him had been only a short interlude.

My mother invited Grandpa and Nanna to Taunton to celebrate my twenty-first birthday, but they had no gas because of rationing, so they could not come. Every year we grandchildren received from Grandpa, without fail, a birthday poem. I received my poem on time, and it touched me so deeply that I have always kept it close by, framed on my bedroom wall.

TWB and Frances
care for a barn owl and its fledgling

Frances (center), sister Rosemary, and brother Robert
with baby woodchucks

TWB with Jimmy Skunk

Frances rides her bike on Hampstead Heath

Thornton W. Burgess III with his daughter Nancy

Fannie Burgess with her granddaughters Frances and Rosemary

Fannie calls TWB to dinner at Laughing Brook

Aunt Sally with skunks and raccoon at the Woodhouse Night Club

TWB with part of his prized bottle collection

TWB and Harrison Cady together late in life, (above) at a
publisher's reception and (below) at Laughing Brook.
In both pictures, TWB is at left.

TO FRANCES
August 22, 1943
Little girl to woman grown
Where have all the seasons flown?
Four of them in every year
Each one leaving you more dear,
Have, uncounted slipping past,
Brought you to this day at last
When, with childish things now done,
Life begins at twenty-one.

Womanhood—the bud full blown
Promises of youth now grown
To maturity that seemed
Dimly distant as we dreamed
In the days of long ago
How in loveliness you'd grow,
Playing hearts as you did then
Only now with hearts of men.

Little girl to woman grown
In my heart there is, I own,
In the joy I share with you
Just a touch of sadness too.
Gone the little girl who crept
Straight into my heart and kept

It forgetful of the years
Sharing in your hopes and fears.

While you're looking forward I
Find I'm looking back, and sigh
For the days when I would feel
Little arms around me steal
And a small voice gave the cue:
"Know what, Grandpa? I love you."
Ah my dear, those days are done;
Love has grown to twenty-one.

Twenty-one! All life before!
God be with and help you o'er
Every stone that blocks your way;
Guard you through each night and day;
Lead you where the flowers blow
And the singing waters flow;
Give you all the fullness of
His deep understanding love.
                    Grandpa

Later he wrote in his diary: "Aug. 25—A nice letter from Frances written on her twenty-first birthday. She is a dear girl, and I think she loves me greatly."

Soon I was to meet an army colonel, William Keel, at the camp. He pursued me with invitations to dinner and dances. I threw myself into this gaiety, but with an empty heart. Six months later he received orders to transfer to Newport News, Virginia. He asked me to marry him and accompany him there. At first I said no, as I did not know him well, did not love him, and was concerned that he was twelve years older than me. Yet he also seemed a kind and thoughtful person who would be a good husband. Daddy-Bill advised me at first not to marry him, but I did not have much respect for my stepfather at this time. Over the years his infidelity to my mother spoiled any positive feelings I might have had toward him. He also suggested to me that when one marries, love flies out the window, so he concluded that it didn't really matter whether I loved Bill Keel or not. I introduced Bill to Grandpa and Nanna, and they thought him a nice, acceptable person to marry if that was my wish.

In Taunton I missed Laughing Brook so much. One day there, as I sat on the grass reading by a flower bed, a sparrow alighted on my shoulder for a moment. It was one more instance of the wonder and surprise that characterized my visits to my grandparents. But I knew I had to find a life of my own and become less dependent on them.

With faint heart, I agreed to marry on January 8, 1944. I immediately moved with my husband to Newport News. My first child, and Grandpa and Nanna's first great-grandchild, Carolyn Frances (Candy) Keel, was born there on December 7, 1944, the third anniversary of the Japanese attack on Pearl Harbor.

Trouble comes to one and all, Be they big or be they small.

During the war, when Grandpa read Walter Lippmann's column in the newspaper depicting the gruesome fighting overseas, he became angry and horrified about the terrible violence and destruction. He often used this quotation by John Galsworthy to represent his own feelings: "Nothing so endangers the fineness of the human heart as the possession of power over others; nothing so corrodes it as the callous or cruel exercise of that power; and the more helpless the creature over whom power is cruelly or callously exercised, the more the human heart is corroded."

Here is a poem he wrote expressing both his abhorrence of war's violence and his hope for the future:

GIVE UNTO US
*With manmade horror, hate, and strife
The very air we breathe is rife;
And peering through the murk ahead
We shudder in unspoken dread*

As chaos, world woe, fear, and doubt
Confuse, encompass us about,
'Til as we strive to count the cost
Our faith in fellow man is lost.

But hark! The children shout at play.
Give unto us, O Lord, we pray
To hear His voice in Galilee—
"Like unto these"—and know that we
If we but to our trust be true
Shall see the world fashioned anew;
Shall see the dreadful turmoil cease,
And birth of universal peace.

For oh it's here in hearts at play
That lies the hope of future day.
The wrongs we've done shall those set right;
The curse of Cain no longer blight

If justice, mercy, clearer light
That will not yield to lust of might
Implanted be and guarded when
We mold the lives of future men.

His point of view stood in marked contrast to the violence and chaos of the period. Yet he possessed great empathy for soldiers who had to fight in the conflict, and sometimes his work offered solace to those who had to face battle. Testifying to this was a letter to Grandpa that arrived from the Pacific theater of operations in 1944. It referred to an illustrated article about Grandpa in the August 1944 issue of *Life* magazine:

> *Until the other night I had never really seen the unknown friend that made my childhood imagination soar to unknown heights. I cannot tell you to what depths my morale had dropped prior to that evening, nor can I say the reason for the low spirits. But I can say they were very low. Then I saw your article in* Life *which set many long forgotten memories in motion, memories of animated wood folk who came to life and spoke; told me of their joy and happiness in living; gave me little bits of philosophy that even today I remember.*
>
> *I spent many hours with "our" friends and know now, as I knew then, that they are as real as the Japanese empire. Many authors have tried to portray their imaginative animated characters as real living symbols. Some have succeeded to a moderate degree. But none have really captured the color, dignity, and beauty of true animation as you have. . . .*
>
> *After I had read your article and spent a few hours just thinking, I felt better. Our friends seemed to parade before me, each telling a little tale of adventure that made me laugh and cry in turn until I was a little boy again*

propped up with one of your books and at peace with the
world. I just had to sit down and humbly write my appre-
ciation and many thanks.

For myself I am Eddie Hardy, 21, aboard one of
Uncle Sam's destroyers, seeing to it that more people like
you can write for more people like me. . .

Grandpa wrote to Eddie immediately, but he never heard
from him again.

When Grandpa's ten-thousandth newspaper story was published in early 1944, the *Springfield Republican* carried the
following editorial comment:

Years ago when Theodore Roosevelt was President and
he was periodically denouncing those with whom he dis-
agreed, one of his famous controversies was with those
whom he called "nature fakers." He protested against
what he termed their romantic inaccurate descriptions of
animals which did things that animals never could do.
Mr. Burgess has observed such a careful regard for the
facts of natural history that, while he has attributed
speech to his animal friends, who certainly know ways to
communicate much to each other, he has escaped bitter
controversies of that sort. Not the least testimony to his
care in this respect and to the accuracy of his observa-
tions is the fact that with the passing years a large part

of his audience—not less than half of it, he reports—has come to be composed of adults.

In a letter of August 15, 1943, old friend and collaborator Harrison Cady acknowledged Grandpa's approaching milestone with a letter:

My dear Thornton,

I am sending under separate cover a little package to be opened on the day you write your ten-thousandth story, and I hope it will convey in some small measure my great appreciation of the splendid task you have done in writing ten thousand Bedtime Stories during the many years past.

As I have read all but about two hundred and fifty of them, I know how well you have done the job and the high quality you have maintained—many of the stories have been instructive, some humorous, some very touching. To cover these extremes is a rare gift.

I only wish that all the children, both young and old, who have followed them could be assembled in one vast group on this your 10,000 story anniversary to salute you, and I also wish that all the little folks of the forest and the meadows might also be assembled to pay you homage for perhaps they in some unseen manner may know how many of their lives you have saved.

I remember you once said your mother wished you might have been a clergyman and I only wish that she might have lived to have seen the great work you have done and I know of no clergyman who has done better or given more happiness to so many.

Yours sincerely,

Harrison

When my husband returned to civilian life after the war, we moved to Worcester, Massachusetts, where my second child, Kathryn Ann ("Kathy") Keel, was born on November 29, 1947. I was glad at last to be near home again where my children and I could be near Grandpa and Nanna.

Grandpa always had time for his great-grandchildren, as he had for us, and he was ready to answer all their questions. My daughter Candy asked him one day, "Grampa, Johnny Chuck has a large hole in the meadow, and there is a big pile of sand in front of it. I like to watch him come out and go inside again, but what is his house like inside?"

I'd rather be frightened With no cause to fear Than fearful of nothing When danger is near.

Grandpa answered with his usual enthusiastic gift for storytelling, "You have sharp eyes, my dear, for Johnny is not always so easily seen. You have discovered a secret. I will tell you how Sammy Jay found out from Peter Rabbit what Johnny Chuck's house is like inside.

145

"One day Sammy Jay saw Peter Rabbit poke his head out from one of Johnny's old houses. Johnny has a habit of moving out and building himself a new house in a different part of the Green Meadow, perhaps because he is afraid too many of his neighbors have found out where he lives. He likes to keep his house a secret. Sometimes Johnny invites Jimmy Skunk to move into his old house when he leaves, but on this day Sammy saw Peter peering out from Johnny's front door.

The simpler things may chance to be The harder they may be to see.

"'Peter,' asked Sammy, 'tell me what it's like down there in Johnny Chuck's house, since I can't go in and see for myself.'

"'Well, said Peter, 'it's a very nice house. I can't understand why Johnny moved out, but he did, so here I am. It makes a good place for me to hide. It has a long tunnel slanting down for quite a distance from that large entrance and then straightening out. Down a little way the tunnel grows smaller. Way down at the farther end is a nice little bedroom with some grass in it. There are one or two other little rooms, and there are two branch tunnels leading up to the surface of the ground, like side or back doorways. These doorways are hidden by long grass. They come in handy in case of danger. Six or eight babies are born down in the little bedroom in the ground and stay there until they are big enough to hunt food for themselves.'"

"'Does Johnny Chuck have any enemies?" Candy asked worriedly.

"Not many, but enough," Grandpa replied with a chuckle. "Reddy Fox, Old Man Coyote, men, and dogs are the worst. When they are little, chucks have to watch out for hawks and Shadow the Weasel. Reddy Fox tries to dig him out of his house sometimes, but Johnny can dig faster, and if he gets cornered, he will fight so hard that a fox or a small dog will be sorry it ever tried to tackle a woodchuck."

My children benefited from the attention of this loving man, and they loved their great-grandfather very much.

Chapter Six

IN 1950 GRANDPA'S LIFE completely changed. Nanna was suffering terribly with rheumatoid arthritis. She was miserable and could barely move. Grandpa worried about her during the cold weather, saying, "Lady dear, next winter we will go to Florida for a while."

On February 16 she spent her seventy-eighth birthday in bed. On February 22 Grandpa shoveled his eighty-foot driveway free of several inches of snow after a storm. The following day he began to lose balance and suffered numbness in his left side and face. He didn't say anything to anyone, but hired someone to shovel the sidewalk. Later he fell in the front room of the house on Washington Road, hitting the table and knocking bottles to the floor. He called the doctor, who came immediately and diagnosed cerebral thrombosis, a mild stroke. The doctor ordered absolute quiet. Grandpa felt helpless, and Lady was too crippled to help him in any way.

My aunt Ruth Johnson (the wife of Uncle Chester, my mother's brother) moved in to care for them. My brother Robert arrived to take care of Grandpa's typing, wired the

Massachusetts Audubon Society to cancel an upcoming lecture, and then canceled all other engagements. He and Nanna received many letters and visits from family and friends, offering as much help and encouragement as possible.

On March 21 Grandpa said, "Lady didn't come down for breakfast as usual. I thought she was just sleeping and didn't want to disturb her. I went up to see if I could take breakfast to her at 9:50, and found her staring at me vacantly. Her right side was paralyzed. I broke down completely."

After a lengthy hospital stay to treat what was diagnosed as a serious stroke, our darling Nanna, who had always cared for us with such loving devotion, was brought home to Hampden. During the months that followed, my mother, Rosemary, Jean, and I spent as much time with them as possible. Even though Nanna had nurses caring for her twenty-four hours a day, there was still much we could do for both her and Grandpa. Robert and I helped with the correspondence and story writing; Jean and her husband, Paul, spent much time there as well. Rosemary, though expecting another child, did the very best she could to support everyone, and my mother became a strong source of stability.

Grandpa prayed for Nanna's recovery, and on good days

Pity the lonely, for deep in the heart Is an ache that no doctor can heal by his art.

he was sure his prayers were being answered. But on the bad days he grieved as he lost hope.

During Nanna's illness, I would walk to the barn where Grandpa now had his studio, as painful arthritis in his knees kept him from climbing the steps to his house on the hill. The sun seemed to always be shining on those early summer mornings, which helped keep up everyone's spirits. I tried to make Grandpa smile and occasionally succeeded. He might suddenly laugh out loud over something I had said or done, and then I would laugh too.

Nanna died on August 16, 1950. Grandpa was grief-stricken. Although he was surrounded by those who loved him—for which he showed considerable gratitude, love, and appreciation—he felt terribly alone. Without Nanna, his Lady, he had neither home nor life. Nothing seemed to matter to him anymore. He wept inconsolably and often during the months that followed.

To make matters worse, in late August, Hurricane Carol caused terrible destruction throughout New England. The brook ran wild, mightily thrashing down from the hills, carrying branches, logs, stones, and even boulders on its way. It tore along the banks, carving out new paths with its raging waters and upending trees, leaving the roots naked. All of Hampden was flooded.

In the fall of that year, one of Nanna's nurses, Katherine Jones, called on Grandpa fairly often, together with her husband, Frank. Soon Frank was offering to do odd jobs for

Grandpa, and Katherine helped about the house when she visited. Grandpa asked them if they would like to spend the winter in his home in Springfield, as he had been invited by his friends, the Barclays, to join them for a month or two in Tobago in the British West Indies, where he could write comfortably without dealing with the cold New England winter. Katherine and Frank agreed.

Before Grandpa left, much work needed to be done, for he was far behind in his story collaborations with Harrison Cady. He had hired a professional secretary to help him catch up, and he welcomed the work as a diversion from his grief.

Finally, on December 29, 1951, my mother and I saw this tired, broken man off on the boat bound for Tobago. "I don't know how I can carry on without Lady," he cried.

By 1953, my marriage to Bill Keel had come to an end. Though he was a good father and a kind man, ours was not a love match. I felt guilt and anxiety about my lack of feeling for him and knew he should be free to find a mutually loving relationship with someone else. Soon after our divorce he remarried, and we remained friends.

I wrote to Grandpa to try to explain the divorce. At first he was shocked and disappointed in me, as I knew he would be, for he did not believe in divorce. He

Whatever you decide to do, Make up your mind to see it through.

151

thought that after my mother's experience, I would never follow such a path. But when I packed up the children and visited him at Laughing Brook, I received his love and understanding, in spite of his disappointment. I returned to Worcester and enrolled as a day student at Clark University while my children attended the Bancroft School. I continued to exchange letters and visits with Grandpa, and he enjoyed the simple gifts I brought him, especially the plum pudding I made for him at Christmas each year.

Although I saw him much less after I was married, and still less after Nanna died, Grandpa's influence continued in my life and in those of my children. He loved every one of his great-grandchildren and was always writing poems to them. Here is one such poem, sent from Tobago in 1958:

FROM THE LAND OF ALWAYS SUMMER
Down here in the Land of Summer
Where Jack Frost can never freeze
Sunbeams and the dancing raindrops
Play together if you please.
Little lizards catch their dinners
On the ceiling overhead.
Fireflies light little lanterns
For me when I go to bed.
Little Tree Frogs, nightly singing,
Like to take a shower too;
Not a teeny wee bit bashful

Love to hop right in with you.
Crabs dig holes in sand to hide in;
Proper place for Crabs to be.
But it sometimes happens that we
See one climbing up a tree.
Merry Little Breezes blowing
In from far across the sea
Send my papers helter-skelter
For the fun of teasing me.
Down here in the Land of Summer
It is lovely, nothing less,
But between us here's a secret—
That I'm homesick I confess.

Until Nanna's death Grandpa had written six stories a week for thirty years. He had never missed a deadline, and—with the exception of just one week, during which the *New York Herald Tribune*'s managing editor decided to withdraw them with the idea of gauging public reaction—his stories had appeared every day but Sunday in this and other nationally read papers for three decades. So great was the volume of cables and letters during that one-week hiatus that before the week was out, the staff at the *Herald Tribune* felt certain that a readership for Grandpa's stories would continue as long as he could write them. In fact, his fan mail was so heavy that much of his time was spent responding to letters not only from the United States and Canada, but from every country where his books were read.

They had been translated into nine foreign languages. Grownups were as apt to write to him as children were.

But in 1960, at the age of eighty-six, Grandpa finally retired from writing newspaper stories, with a total of over fifteen thousand to his credit, written over nearly half a century. In 1964 the Boston Museum of Science honored Grandpa with a special citation and gold medal at the initial Bradford Washburn Award ceremonies. Washburn designated Grandpa as one of the three men who had most influenced his choice of career, as he had first become interested in nature by reading Burgess stories. "He was a giant for us," Washburn said years later. "He contributed an enormous amount to people of my era. Whatever can be done to deify the man is a good idea. He was a hell of a lot more than a nice guy. He was warm. He was a marvelous man. You empathized with him immediately." The citation hailed him as "the Pied Piper who led generations of children down the path to the wide, wonderful world out-of-doors."

Laughing Brook changed drastically after my grandmother died. Katherine Jones took on some of Grandpa's typing. Eventually he asked her and Frank to live with him permanently, which they agreed to do. Frank helped take care of both Laughing Brook and the house in Springfield, which was a great relief to Grandpa. When the 1955 hurricane turned Laughing Brook into a raging river once again, washing away the garage and collapsing one side of the barn,

Frank rebuilt the barn with help from a good neighbor, Dalton Philpott, adding a new studio to the barn. In 1958 Grandpa sold his house in Springfield, as the house and barn in Hampden had been winterized and he and the Joneses were living there year-round.

As his caretakers, Frank and Katherine wanted to move Grandpa and Nanna's things out and move their things in. My mother and we grandchildren, though we could understand this wish, were not too happy about it. For one thing, we were not sure where the removed articles were to be stored. Grandpa grew very close to the Joneses, and they began doing everything together, calling themselves the trio. He took them to Arizona on his trips there and afforded them the opportunity to go on their own while he was in Tobago, because Frank had asthma and the climate of the Southwest was good for him. He took them to Tobago once, too. Grandpa was wonderful to them, and they were good companions and help to him as well. Also during these years, my young brother William began to visit Grandpa a great deal, and Grandpa grew very fond of him.

He lives best who will arrange His way of life to constant change.

Because Grandpa couldn't live at Laughing Brook by himself anymore, we were grateful to the Joneses for enabling him to continue on there. My mother and I went to Tobago to visit him two or three times, and we all went back to

Laughing Brook as much as we could. But it was different. He deferred to the Joneses more and more, and I felt a pinch of jealousy. Nevertheless, Grandpa and I continued a close and loving relationship.

In 1963, Grandpa suffered a stroke and had to be confined to the Mary Lyons Nursing Home in Hampden. Then Frank Jones died in March 1964. Katherine was left alone and couldn't take care of herself or the house anymore. Everything fell into a sorry state.

Grandpa and I spoke of the situation at Laughing Brook and of the loneliness Katherine was suffering since Frank's death and Grandpa's departure. Grandpa had come to think of her almost as a granddaughter. He felt a deep compassion for her but did not know how to take good care both of her and of his property. Finally, my mother consulted with Grandpa's conservator, and it was decided that they would help Katherine find another place to live and find a caretaker for the property.

Letters constituted a lifeline for him at the nursing home. Mail still came in from all parts of the globe, and he kept busy at least three days each week dictating replies. Ernestine Johnson (no relation to my mother's family) helped him answer every letter. Attired in white shirt, bow tie, and trousers, and sitting erect in his wheelchair in front of a small work table, Grandpa never lost his dignity. Ernestine observed Grandpa's fortitude day by day, and she described him as lonely yet concealing his despair by continuing to write cre-

atively, which helped maintain his spirit and an optimistic outlook. If the following letter to my daughter Kathy, dated
March 28, 1964, is any indication, he kept his sense of
humor and attitude of kindness throughout this difficult time:

> Dear Kathy,
>
> What did you think of your old grandpa with his silly
> laughter? I know you will be happy to learn that he grad-
> uated from the parallel bars to the wheelchair, from the
> wheelchair to the walker, and he is doing very well with it.
>
> It did me a world of good seeing you, my dear, and I
> hope it won't be so long before I see you again.
>
> I can't write myself or even typewrite, but a very dear
> friend has volunteered to do my typing. I hope your
> Easter was a very happy one.
>
> My love to mother and Candy with very much to your
> precious self!
>
> Grampa

Ernestine said she enjoyed Grandpa's wit and considerate
behavior. "But," she added, "it seemed he always was looking
out the window toward town, wishing that neighbors would
drop by for a visit. When they did, he always welcomed them
and treated them as his most esteemed guests; but for the
most part, perhaps he was so famous and successful that
townspeople were afraid he might not receive them in his present condition. There was often the tiny knock on the door,

however, as a youngster came to seek aid for an injured animal or sick bird. Mr. Burgess would stop whatever he was doing and give the child and the hurt creature his total attention."

The ups and downs of Grandpa's last months were chronicled, as always, in letters to his dear friend Harrison Cady, of which these are excerpts:

April 18, 1964

Dear Harrison,

Now that spring is really here I suspect you are kicking up your heels and forgetting all about years. I am not exactly kicking up my heels yet but I'm going to.

At present one heel is anchored with a brace. I know you are anxious to hear from [me] as to how I'm getting on.

I'm getting there step by step and it takes a whole lot of them but there is satisfaction after I look back.

I know you'll be interested in the fact that I received a letter from Little, Brown, stating that the book I sent them last year is already in the works and will be out this year. Also the Canadian publishers have brought out a new and very attractive edition of 10 of the bedtime stories. Also last month or late in February I had a record released bearing two stories in my own voice. The record was made last June! So that is not too bad for 90 and I'm beginning to think of another book! . . .

Here at the home I'm seeing a lot of real old age and I'm glad that we are no older than we are. I'm more than ever convinced that years have little to do with age!

We young fellows have to show what we can do. . . .

You know my name so I'm signing this with my initials.

TWB

August 29, 1964

Dear Harrison,

I love that last letter head of yours with Grandfather Frog tipping his hat to the flowers. But then I love all of your drawings. . . .

Yes, Harrison, the world has been good to us! Very good. I think we both appreciate this fact.

For my part I am finding old age quite as interesting as any other period in a long life!

I still feel that if I had my life to live over again I would ask for little change! . . .

So as you say around the track we go! And the flag isn't in sight yet!

Yours with very much affection,

Thornton

Grandpa was deeply touched when, in the early spring of 1964, his son Thornton came to Hampden to see him after many years of absence. Thornton also spent a few days with Mildred and his three children. Then, shortly after his return to Granada Hills, California, in May of that year, Thornton died suddenly of a heart attack at the age of fifty-seven. Ernestine had to bring the terrible news to Grandpa, who by this time was seriously ailing himself.

Loyalty is priceless and
Is neither sold nor bought.
Alas, how few who seem to know
Its value as they ought.

In May 1965 Katherine Jones succumbed in an early-morning flash fire, one day after moving into a three-room home in East Longmeadow, Massachusetts. Ernestine again was the bearer of bad tidings. "He took it rather well as I told him," she said, "but when I returned to his bedside later in the day, it was clear he had cried to himself." At this time, Grandpa was very tired, suffering from cancer of the throat and approaching his own death. He died on June 5, 1965.

Harrison Cady outlived him by five years and died in New York City on December 9, 1970, at the age of ninety-three.

In his public life, my grandfather was often recognized for the profound and positive influence he exerted as a storyteller and naturalist. An editorial in the Sunday *New York Herald*

Tribune was typical of the critical reception he received throughout his career:

> *How deep does human education by vivid fiction go? It must arrive at good, one feels sure, when it is so honest as that of Mr. Burgess. He makes the animals no more deceptively human than our ignorance of their talk and meditations and motives obliges him to do. Defects in the amiability of Grandfather Frog and Hooty are not permitted to appear as moral flaws. They have to eat what they can and neither pity nor family affection restrains their hunger; but they do not kill as weasels, cats, and men and women do, for perverse pleasure.*
>
> *Such straightforward ethics and natural science, though, would never account entirely for the reality and poetry of the cosmos illumined by Mr. Burgess, now here, now there, from day to day. He feels in his own bones the desperate mercy of the winter sleep, the delicate delight of early spring, the pleasures of having enough to eat in summer, the loneliness and uncertainty of a young animal's first autumn. He makes the hasty reader even feel these with such primordial intensity that many probably would say that they are better men for having briefly been Johnny Chuck.*

Grandpa counted a British queen, Elizabeth II, and at least one U.S. president, Teddy Roosevelt, among his admir-

ers. He in turn considered Roosevelt a great environmentalist and conservationist, and the two men corresponded for
many years. Political officeholders aren't allowed to receive
gifts, but Roosevelt once told Grandpa, "Your books,
Burgess, I can and am proud to receive."

Bradford Washburn, the founding father of Boston's
Museum of Science, wrote Grandpa, "As you know, your
wonderful books had a tremendous effect on my love of
nature as a youngster. My mother and father read them to me
from the time I could understand anything until the time I
could read. And I read them avidly myself as virtually the first
English prose that I tackled alone. There is also not the
slightest doubt in any of our minds here at the Museum that
these books had the same effect on literally millions of
American youngsters throughout two full generations."

Such acclaim has continued over the years. In the
September 1983 issue of *Audubon* magazine, Olin S.
Pettingell, Jr., spoke of Paul Brooks's "perceptive book"
Speaking for Nature. Brooks, former editor in chief at
Houghton Mifflin's trade book division, said he considered
Thornton Burgess, John Burroughs, and Ernest Thompson
Seton "old-fashioned naturalists who dealt with wild nature
as an endlessly fascinating and romantic subject."

*They attained fame before radio had come into its own
and long before television, when the written word was the
principal medium for mass communication. I liked books*

by both Burroughs and Seton. But they were books appearing only now and then, and soon read. The Burgess stories came regularly in newspapers, leading me on from day to day. The more of his stories I read, the more I became interested in the author himself. I clipped out every item I spotted about him in newspapers or magazines and pasted it in my steadily enlarging scrapbooks of Burgess stories. I felt that any man who could write as he did must be worth knowing. Today I remember Thornton W. Burgess as a popular figure admired for his accomplishments in educating young people about nature and conservation, and I remember him as a person warmhearted, entertaining, and outgoing. As, just as important, I remember him with everlasting gratitude for introducing me early in life to the natural world that has given me so much satisfaction ever since.

Recently, when I visited Paul Brooks at his home in Lincoln, Massachusetts, he confirmed this estimation of Grandpa and his work. Still, my favorite accolade was published in the *Herald Tribune*, affirming that "many probably would say that they are better men for having briefly been Johnny Chuck."

Grandpa did not leave a large estate, as some have imagined. This suggests just how much of his personal wealth had already been given away to family, friends, and worthwhile causes.

After his death, the Massachusetts Audubon Society, in cooperation with the Hampden Lions Club, purchased the eighteen
acres of Laughing Brook "to create a memorial to
the late writer and to influence future generations." The idea of opening a wildlife
sanctuary there had come from Grandpa
himself, according to Allen Morgan,   *'Twill do no harm*
executive vice president of the Massa-   *to wish, for you*
chusetts Audubon Society. Grandpa   *Will find some*
had written, "I would like to leave the   *wishes do come*
property in trust to an organiza-   *true.*
tion. . . . It would require a mainte-
nance fund which I'm not in a position
to supply. . . . All of this, of course, is an 'Old
Man's Dream,' but I like to think it possible if not probable."

The land around Laughing Brook has been increased by
Massachusetts Audubon to 354 acres and contains many
beautiful, well-marked trails. A new building has been erected
to facilitate programs for children and adults, teachers and
naturalists. It provides teacher training to serve schools in the
Springfield area. Doug Kimball, the director, is ensuring the
education of today's children in the field of natural science,
and the original house is maintained as a museum. A special
fund has been designated to raise money for restoration of the
outbuildings and maintenance.

In 1976, the Thornton W. Burgess Society in Sandwich
was founded by Nancy Titcomb of East Sandwich as a non-

profit educational organization to honor the memory of Grandpa and to carry on his work "to inspire reverence for wildlife and concern for the natural environment." It has established a museum in the 1756 Deacon Eldred house (his aunt Arabella's house) in the town center and the Green Briar Nature Center, which offers natural history classes, nature walks, lectures, and workshops, with a fifty-seven-acre conservation area.

Because of Grandpa's influence and that of other early conservationists, many elementary and secondary schools have begun featuring environmental studies. Scott Stein, chairman of the science department of Springside School for girls in Chestnut Hill, Philadelphia—where Grandpa lectured once or twice and my two daughters graduated— has developed a remarkable environmental education program. It is designed for pre-kindergarten through grade twelve, "to give the girls the opportunity to investigate their natural world . . . and to give them the scientific environmental literacy and problem-solving capabilities that will all be necessary in the twenty-first century." To facilitate this program, the school is strategically located on a plateau between two streams emptying into the Wissahickon Valley Creek, allowing the girls continuous study and enjoyment of the many natural habitats directly surrounding the school.

These are some of the ways in which Grandpa's legacy has continued for everyone to enjoy. But outside the public realm, his influence has continued throughout my life as his granddaughter, and I have especially appreciated his wisdom during my times of hardship. Before Grandpa's death, two years after my divorce in 1953, I married for the second time, to a childhood friend, and moved to Chestnut Hill in Philadelphia. But soon it was evident that my husband was a victim of the plague called alcoholism, and although we sought help in this predicament there seemed to be no solution to the problem. Sadly we separated. I felt deeply flawed by my apparent inability to give my children a happy and secure home, but managed to persevere and make a new life for myself.

I wish Grandpa could have known that, at last, I found my way into a happy and long-lived marriage. I married Charles Hubbard Meigs in 1968, after Grandpa's death, and am writing this book in our thirtieth year together. Between us we have nineteen grandchildren.

While living in Philadelphia in the 1970s, after my children were grown, some friends and I started teaching an ecology program in the Philadelphia schools under the auspices of the Schuylkill Valley Nature Center. The teachers and the school administration were enthusiastic, and it was a very successful venture. We taught in the classrooms and studied ecosystems in the streets, investigating the cracks in the walks where weeds and ailanthus trees would grow and watching the incessant activities of the ants. We brought the students to the nature center for field trips, where we dipped sieves into the pond to see what we could discover. We walked the trails, dug in the earth to find specimens, and quietly listened for the sounds of the forest. I felt I was following in Grandpa's footsteps. He had always said, "Time outdoors can nurture a deep concern for the natural world. Formal learning about environmental problems such as endangered species has a value, but the experience of picking up a turtle in the woods offers a vastly different way of appreciating our connections with the world."

In 1983 and 1984 I returned to school and earned my teaching certificate in religion at Chestnut Hill College. Grandpa had instilled in me a strong sense of wonder about the strange yet beautiful works of creation. Why in the world did God create billions of stars with only one planet Earth to sustain human life? Why did He create millions of eggs to beget only one frog? Why was there such a paradox of cruelty and compassion, hate and love, good and evil, right and wrong, in human existence? My discussions with Grandpa sprouted the seeds of my own studies and contemplative thoughts in this area.

Grandpa liked to joke that "Success is attaining a position in life where people tell you you're a lot smarter than you know you are." By any standard, his life's work was a success, though he remained quite humble about his achievements.

Grandpa ended his autobiography with a quotation from Proverbs: "Let another man praise thee and not thine own mouth; a stranger and not thine own lips."

These words of mine are only a few of many words of praise sung for Thornton W. Burgess. His dream was fulfilled. His legacy continues.

Epilogue

$\mathcal{N}$OT HAVING VISITED Laughing Brook for many years after Grandpa's death, I returned in the summer of 1991, feeling a bit anxious about what I might find. The Massachusetts Audubon Society now owned the property, and I knew that the organization had little money to maintain the buildings. Nevertheless, I was unprepared for the feeling of loss that overcame me as I drove toward the house. The sky was bare of the great sheltering elms, which once had stood so high. The house looked vulnerable and naked.

As I had come unannounced, I could not visit inside the main house, where on the first floor many pieces of Grandpa and Nanna's eighteenth-century furniture still stood, together with some original paintings by Harrison Cady, the original edition of *The Bride's Primer,* and other memorabilia, including Nanna's conch shell. I discovered the house locked; the window boxes beneath every window, which Nanna had filled with pink geraniums, were empty; the joyous, bountiful kitchen at the north end of the house had been torn down; and the guest house, Grandpa's house on the hill, and the old barn and studio, overflowing with memories, were marked with signs reading "Unsafe" and "Do Not Enter." I was barred the place that, more than any other, had been my home.

The vegetable gardens and the cornfield lay fallow; the flower gardens were grassed over; the well sweep with its wooden bucket was gone. An overgrowth of trees was obliterating the western meadow, where cicadas and crickets and katydids had cast a spell with their bewitching cadences and where fireflies had filtered through the grasses, shining intermittent phosphorescent lights to brighten the twilight. I felt as lonely and abandoned as the farm seemed to be. I turned to leave.

But then I heard the brook. Ever-changing but constant, life-giving, flowing through seasons of fullness and drought, sunshine and rain, living and dying, the brook had endured. I hurried toward the sound of running water. Its currents sparkled in the sun and filled me with delight.

Sitting alone on the green grassy bank, I heard the flutelike notes of a thrush close by. I watched and listened as the brook surged over the rocks, catching and reflecting the sunbeams, a mirrorlike sheet of water fanning white on either side and cascading over rocks, splashing, whirling into small pools of sparkling lights, dancing over smooth brown pebbles, sounding a joyful laughter. How swift and full it ran; how steadily it rolled along the edges of fields and marshes, tumbling down from the "purple hills," creating "smiling pools." I lay back on the grassy bank, warmed by "jolly round red Mr. Sun," and looked up at the "blue, blue sky."

As I lay there by the brook, I distinctly heard the sound of Nanna's conch shell calling me. It was lunch time, and I wanted to hurry to the house to be with everyone there. I could see my grandfather coming down those rough stepping stones from the hill, and my heart grew full, knowing he was going to extol the talents of my grandmother's cooking and make us all feel that we were the most special people on earth.

MY GARDEN
Last summer filled with roses
And other blooms galore.
My garden now is empty—
A memory of yore.

'Tis desolate and dreary.
Its broken stalks are sere,
Its onetime fragrant beauty
Gone with the yesteryear.

It lies there stark and frozen,
Each former lovely bed
Now covered with a blanket
Of leaves all brown and dead.

No single winsome blossom
Can anywhere be found.

No hint of future glory
  Doth show above the ground.

But still I love my garden,
  So frozen, bleak and bare,
For well I know my flowers
  Are safely sleeping there.

  Thornton W. Burgess
  Winter 1937

Sources

In lieu of a formal bibliography or footnotes, the author offers the following partial list of sources which helped supplement her own memory and understanding of Thornton W. Burgess. All references to Burgess's diaries are courtesy of the Thornton W. Burgess Society.

Page

4   "Its phrases": Rachel Carson, "An Island I Remember" in Paul Brooks, *The House of Life*, Boston: Houghton Mifflin, 1972.

10   "In those days" and subsequent references from Burgess's autobiography: Thornton W. Burgess, *Now I Remember*, Boston: Little, Brown, 1960.

22   *Old Mother West Wind*, Boston: Little, Brown, 1910.

29   *The Burgess Bird Book for Children*, Boston: Little, Brown, 1919.

34   "In this busy world": William Hornaday speech, courtesy Thornton W. Burgess Society, Sandwich, Mass.

56   "Dear Alfred": Correspondence with Dr. Alfred Gross, courtesy Bowdoin College Library, Brunswick, Me.

62   "Few light moments": Daniel, Hawthorne, *Federal Judge Harold Medina, A Biography*, New York: W. Funk, 1952.

66   "Aunt Sally": Burgess, Thornton W., *Aunt Sally's Friends in Fur*, Boston: Little, Brown, 1955.

Index